..."AND THE LAST SHALL BE FIRST"

Native Policy in an Era of Cutbacks

..."AND THE LAST SHALL BE FIRST"

Native Policy in an Era of Cutbacks

Murray Angus

NC Press Limited
Toronto 1991

CANADIAN MENNONITE UNIVERSITY
LIBRARY
500 SHAFTESBURY BLVD
WINNIPEG, MANITOBA
CANADA R3P 2N2

> Front cover: Norval Morriseau 1931 -
> **THE LAND (Landrights) 1976**
> acrylic on canvas
> 122.0 x 96.7 cm
> McMichael Canadian Art Collection
> Gift of Mr. and Mrs. Richard H. Bak
> 1982.6
> Used with the permission of the artist.

©Aboriginal Rights Coalition, 1990
Revised Edition, 1991

No part of this publication may be reproduced, stored in a retrieval system, or transmitted, in any form or by any means, electronic, mechanical, photocopying, recording or otherwise, without the prior written permission of NC Press Limited.

Editing and Design: Cathleen Kneen

Canadian Cataloguing in Publication Data

Angus, Murray, 1950 -
". . . And The Last Shall Be First"
Native Policy in an Era of Cutbacks

Rev. ed.
Includes bibliographical references.
ISBN 1-55021-064-5

1. Canada – Native races. 2. Indians of North America – Canada – Claims. *3. Indians of North America – Canada – Legal status, laws, etc. 4. Inuit – Canada – Claims.* 5. Inuit – Canada – Legal Status, laws, etc.* 6. Métis – Claims.* 7. Métis – Legal status, laws, etc. I. Title.

E92.A54 1991   323.1'197071   C91-094091-6

We would like to thank the Ontario Arts Council and the Canada Council for their assistance in the production of this book.

New Canada Publications, a division of NC Press Limited, Box 452, Station A, Toronto, Ontario, Canada, M5W 1H8.

Distributed in the United States of America by Seven Hills Books Distributors, 49 Central Ave., Cincinnati, Ohio 45202.

Printed and bound in Canada

CONTENTS

ACKNOWLEDGMENTS

FORWORD

INTRODUCTION   1

PART 1: THE CONTEXT OF CUTBACKS

The Fiscal Crisis   7
The Political Challenges of Cutting Back   12
The Conservative Agenda in Action   16

PART 2: ". . . AND THE LAST SHALL BE FIRST"
NATIVE POLICY IN AN ERA OF CUTBACKS

The Position of Native People in Canadian Society   23
The Nielsen Report: *Laying the Groundwork for Cuts*   24
Expenditure Reductions: *Nielsen By Another Name*   28
Self-Government: *The Real Buffalo Jump of the 1990s?*   31
The Constitutional Process: *"Embroiling the Provinces"*   35
Specific Claims: *What Price, Honour?*   38
Comprehensive Claims: *One Step Forward, Two Steps Back*   44
Amazon North?: *The Continuing Loss of Native Lands*   51
Going to Court: *Certain Costs, Uncertain Benefits*   56
"As Long As The Sun Shines. . .":
    The Current Conjuncture for Native People   62
Of Guns and Feathers: *The Indian Summer of 1990*   64

PART 3: THE FUTURE OF NON-NATIVE RESPONSE

From Support to Solidarity   71
The Role of an Aboriginal Rights Coalition   74

ENDNOTES   77

INDEX   85

ACKNOWLEDGEMENTS

I wish to express my appreciation to Catherine Shapcott, who edited and supervised the production of the First Edition, and to Cathleen Kneen of NC Press whose enthusiasm for the project was instrumental in making this Revised Edition a reality.

I remain indebted to the following people for their encouragement and support during the preparation of the first edition of this book: Iain Angus, Elaine Bishop, Tony Clarke, Peter DiGangi, Gordon DiGiacomo, Barbara Foley, Vince Greason, Peter Hamel, Morley Hanson, Patrick Kellerman, Marion and Pat Kerans, Michael McBane, Virginia Mooney, John Olthuis, Lorna Schwartzentruber, Norman Sponchia, Deb Stienstra, Andy Tamas, Roger Townshend, and above all . . .

Maureen Kellerman

This book originated as a project of **The Aboriginal Rights Coalition (Project North)**, an ecumenical coalition of national churches, church bodies, and regional groups working in solidarity with First Nations.

FOREWORD

With the collapse of the First Ministers Conferences on aboriginal rights in 1987, the Canadian churches initiated a critical review of their responsibilities in advocating justice for Canada's aboriginal people.

Throughout the 1970s and 1980s, the churches actively supported struggles for aboriginal justice through Project North (now the Aboriginal Rights Coalition). During this period, Project North developed public education and action strategies in support of aboriginal concerns, including the impacts of mega-energy developments in the North, federal policies on comprehensive land claims, and the entrenchment of native self-government in the Canadian Constitution.

By the mid-1980s, it was becoming clear that major structural changes were taking place in Canada's economy and society. The social welfare state, which had been developed in Canada since the Second World War, was gradually being dismantled. The corresponding erosion of federal social programs was bound to have a direct impact on Canada's aboriginal people.

To better understand this new political conjuncture and the challenges of aboriginal justice, the interim committee responsible for the future directions of Project North commissioned Murray Angus to do a study. More specifically, Murray was asked to prepare a background paper to address three sets of concerns and questions:

(1) Identify some of the forces underlying the dismantling of the social welfare state in Canada;

(2) Clarify some of the corresponding shifts in federal policies and programs affecting aboriginal people;

(3) Outline some of the implications of these trends for solidarity work with aboriginal people by churches and non-native groups.

The document that follows accomplishes all three tasks. It provides fresh understandings and new insights concerning the challenges and demands for aboriginal justice in Canada today. It also provides a framework for developing mission priorities and action strategies in solidarity with aboriginal people in the 1990s.

There is no escaping the moral and political message of this study – namely, "... *The Last Shall Be First*". The 'last' to be admitted to the social welfare state were certainly among the 'first' to be hit by the recent wave of cutbacks in social programs. But this theme has a deeper historical significance. The 'first' people of this land are still the 'last' to benefit from the building of Canada itself.

Perhaps the best hope for the future lies in the building of a democratic social movement, which would link aboriginal organizations, labour unions, church groups, women's associations, farm organizations, environmental groups, peace networks, anti-poverty groups, and senior citizens associations. This movement would develop a new social contract in this country to ensure that "the last shall be the first" to benefit.

Tony Clarke
Chair, Justice and Peace Commission
Canadian Council of Churches

INTRODUCTION

"The Tories are looking for ways to get out of the Native business." This was the blunt, but considered, opinion of one close observer (a former ministerial aide) of the Native scene during the process of consultation leading up to this book.

This book is about *why* the Tories want to get out of the Native business, and about *how* they are doing so on a wide variety of policy fronts. It is written for ordinary "white" Canadians who want to understand more about Native issues, and also about their own economic and political situation in these turbulent times. The focus may be Native issues, but the issues are social and economic policy, and the relationship of middle class Canadians to these policies. A connection *does exist* between what is happening to Native people in Canada today, and what is happening to the rest of us, particularly in the middle class; knowing this connection is important because it can allow us to act in more politically and ethically responsible ways.

This book does not provide a Native perspective on current policy issues. If one wants to learn about Native culture, history, present-day concerns, worldviews, aspirations, or whatever, one can – and should – consult the authentic voices of Native peoples themselves, available through a wide variety of media in Canada today.

This is a book about Native policy, or, more precisely, about the policies of the government which represents us in our dealing with Native peoples in Canada. It is, after all, *our* governments that have had most of the control over the relations between Natives and non-Natives in our society. It is our governments that have decided in the past how much land would be given to newcomers, and how much would be left for Indians, Inuit or Métis. It is our governments that have determined what access Native peoples would have to resources necessary for their own development. It is our governments that determined what rules would have to be followed by Native peoples if they wanted to assert their rights – or even it they should be allowed to do so. It is our governments that decided what limits would be put on Native peoples' freedom to travel, gamble, drink, fish, hunt, trap, sell pulpwood, exchange goods amongst themselves, trade with others, speak their own language, organize, own and control property. In short, it is our governments that have had most of the power to decide what place Native people would have in our society.

2 AND THE LAST SHALL BE FIRST

It is also appropriate for non-Native Canadians to concentrate their attention on the government because it is the government which is accountable *to us*. As non-Native Canadians, we have no right to be involved in the internal decision-making processes of aboriginal groups; what they decide, and how they decide it, is their own business. With the government, however, we *do* have the right – indeed, an obligation – to ensure that it acts on our behalf in the ways which we want. After all, it represents *us* when it makes laws which affect the relationship between ourselves and aboriginal people in Canada.

This book provides the non-Native reader with an overview of how our government has been dealing with Native peoples over the last twenty years in Canada. It describes events and decisions on a variety of policy fronts – land claims, self-government, the constitution, funding, the law, etc. It argues, however, that the government's actions in all of these areas has come to be dominated by one, overriding objective: its desire to "get out of the Native business".

There are several reasons for this objective: *First*, Native problems are seen by many politicians as intractable, meaning no amount of federal effort will ever achieve the desired results. Politically, then, they represent a "no-win" set of issues for a government, that is, Ottawa will never be able to do enough to satisfy Native demands, and the "pay-off" at the polls would never amount to much if they did. As one former Minister of Indian Affairs put it: "There is no reward: it is a black hole."[1]

Second, the responsibility of serving Native people, as required by Section 91(24) of the British North America (BNA) Act, is bureaucratically complex. As the Nielsen Report on Indians and Natives noted in 1985: "The effect ... has been the creation of a department of the federal government which has attempted to provide a full array of federal, provincial and municipal services to status Indians".[2] Maintaining such a monolithic department would not be consistent with the Tories' decentralist approach to governing; nor would it fit with its determined efforts to "downsize" the federal bureaucracy.

Finally, there are *economic* reasons why the government would like to extract itself from its established obligations: simply put, Native programming is expensive, and threatens to be more so in the years ahead. Any government anxious to control its overall spending, as the Conservatives are determined to do (at least on certain fronts), will therefore have a strong incentive for wanting to escape from its traditional obligations to Native people.

While the attitudes described above are important influences on the government policies, they do not provide a complete explanation for recent trends in Native policy. In many respects, they represent (however accurately) only the attitudes of politicians and bureaucrats towards Native issues when these issues are viewed in *isolation*. But it must be remembered that Native policies are not developed in complete isolation from other issues; on the contrary, they are developed within a much broader policy environment which is often shaped by factors quite unrelated to Native people themselves. To treat Native policies as separate from everything else government does, and to respond to them on that basis, is to condemn oneself to forever fighting brushfires in the battle for justice.

What, then, is the broader context? Since the mid-1970s, and especially since the Conservatives took office in 1984, the policy-making environment in Canada has been dominated by an overriding concern for "fiscal restraint". This quest for "fiscal restraint" has become – and will continue to be – the predominant factor shaping the government's policies towards Native people.

This book analyzes what lies behind this current preoccupation of governments – how and when the pursuit of "fiscal restraint" began, what political choices contributed to it, how governments have responded to it, and how Native people are being affected by it. This analysis demonstrates that ordinary middle-class, "white" Canadians are not as far removed from the policies affecting Native peoples as they might assume. The success of the government's agenda for achieving "fiscal restraint" in general, and for "getting out of the Native business" in particular, will hinge largely on the amount of political support it can cultivate from the middle class in Canada. Clarifying our position in relation to the government's agenda will help us to make informed choices about our own political response.

Part 1:

The Context of Cutbacks

The Context of Cutbacks

The Fiscal Crisis

The post-war era saw a radical transformation of the government's role in Canadian society. Buoyed by an expanding economy and supported by the new economic theories of Keynes, the government assumed a more activist role in the management of the country's social and economic affairs.

An important indicator of this increased involvement was the growth of government expenditures. In the three decades following the war, total government spending as a percentage of Gross National Expenditure (GNE) rose from 22.1 per cent in 1950 to 41.3 per cent in 1975.[3] What characterized these expenditures was not just that they increased continually over a 25-year period, but that they grew in two directions at once.[4]

One significant new area of expenditure growth was subsidies to business. These included not only direct grants to private companies, but also the provision of publicly financed services and facilities designed to reduce the production costs of the private sector (highways, ports, airports, public utilities, research and development facilities, marketing boards, facilities for education and training). By 1985, the Nielsen Report on Services and Subsidies to Business could identify more than 200 federal or federal/provincial programs designed to assist and support the private sector in Canada. The estimated annual cost of such services by 1984 was $16.4 billion.[5]

The other significant new area of spending during the post-war era was social programs. As Moscovitch notes, these programs served a dual function. On the one hand, they were meant to support the post-war policy of full employment "through a range of education, employment, family and child support and family regulation policies." On the other hand, they were intended to "deal with a relatively wide range of society's casualties"[6] through unemployment insurance (1952), old age security (1952), disability pensions (1954), hospital insurance (1958), medicare (1966), and social assistance (1966). Overall spending on health, education, and income security rose from 8.2 per cent of GNE in 1950, to 23 per cent in 1976.[7]

The continual growth of government spending in these areas was made possible by the rapid expansion of the country's economy. An expanding economy meant increased tax revenues for governments, both from corporations and workers who benefited from high levels of employment. This expansion of the tax base enabled the government to increase its expenditures in two directions at once over a 20-year period.

By the late 1960s, several factors in the international economy began to converge which undermined the government's ability to continue spending in both directions at once. The dominance of the North American (United States) economy in the global capitalist system had peaked; by the mid-1960s, the productive capacities of its traditional competitors (Japan and Western Europe) had recovered from their war-time destruction and were providing renewed competition on world markets.[8] This increased competition contributed to a decline in the rate of growth in both the American and Canadian economies.

A reduced rate of economic growth had implications both for government revenues and expenditures. As the rate of corporate expansion declined, so did the growth in revenues from corporate taxation. A rise in unemployment also affected the government's revenues and expenditures. It meant fewer people were earning an income that could be taxed; it also meant more people were dependent upon state programs such as unemployment insurance and welfare, causing an increase in federal spending.

While the growth rate in the economy was showing signs of decline, another factor in the international economy began to have an impact on government revenue and spending. As a result of post-war advances in technology, particularly in the fields of transportation and communications, it was becoming increasingly possible for private corporations to organize their production activities on a global rather than national scale.[9]

This change in the structure of production marked the beginning of a new phase in the historical development of capitalism,[10] which will have enormous implications for Canadian society. With it, will come a new "international division of labour," with labour-intensive production increasingly assigned to Third World countries where wages and other costs of production are low, and high-tech capital intensive activities assigned to developed economies where wages and other costs remain high. The bargaining power achieved by workers within the regulatory confines of individual nation-states in the post-war era has been dramatically undermined by capital's newfound ability to go elsewhere.

This new phase of global capitalism has also had implications for the role of the State in countries such as Canada. The post-war boom, which gave rise to the welfare state, was predicated in part on a tacit "accommodation" between capital and labour.[11] In this unstated pact, labour's right to organize was conceded, as long as capital retained its traditional "right" to make investment decisions according to its own best interests. The role of the State was to "manage" the relationship between these relatively equal antagonists, in the overall interests of a smooth-running national economy.

As capital increasingly breaks free from individual nation-states, the role of the State changes. Governments no longer have the ability to manage capital to the degree once possible. Because of capital's ability to relocate in search of higher profit margins, the State – to the extent it chooses to rely on private capital – is reduced to competing for it with other nations. The State's function shifts from managing the internal relationship between capital and labour to competing for investment capital on a global scale.

Governments compete for this capital by providing a "profitable investment climate." The factors that contribute to such a climate include: reduced government regulation over investment decisions, corporate concentration, environmental protection, health and safety, and plant closings; restrictions on the ability of workers to bargain collectively, which contributes to a downward pressure on wages; reduced social security programs to induce workers to accept low-paying jobs; and the implementation of tight money policies, to protect the value of investments rather than workers' jobs. Factors of special significance to this book are: lower tax rates and an increase in other direct and indirect financial incentives to industry – direct grants, tax breaks and the provision of a publicly financed infrastructure.

The impact of these structural changes in the global economy began to be felt in Canada by the early 1970s. On the one hand, the government was faced with rising costs in each of its traditional areas of spending. This stemmed from the need to provide business with greater incentives to invest and from the growing demand placed upon social programs as a result of rising unemployment. On the other hand, the government's revenue base was being eroded because of its growing "need" to reduce the tax burden on corporations, and because fewer Canadians were earning an income that could be taxed.

This trend toward steadily rising expenditures against the backdrop of declining revenues represented the beginning of a "fiscal crisis" for the State.[12] This fiscal crisis signalled the end of the era when the government could afford to keep spending increasing amounts in two directions at once. A new era was emerging, marked by growing competition for the government's limited resources.

The Trudeau government's response to this fiscal crisis during the 1970s had four main thrusts:

First, it continued to meet the growing demands of the corporate sector for subsidies, but it began to rely increasingly on the tax system to do it. In addition to lowering the tax rates for corporations,[13] the government made increasing use of "tax expenditures"[14] in the 1970s. This method of providing support to business offered distinct advantages to both parties. For government, they were less visible than grants and other forms of direct expenditures: tax expenditures didn't show up in the Public Accounts.[15] For companies, support came with few performance requirements attached.[16] The shift toward the use of tax expenditures is evident: in 1964, corporate tax incentives were 37 per cent of corporate taxes collected; by 1975, they had risen to 69 per cent. Public revenue lost through fast write-offs grew five times between 1970 and 1975. By 1984, the annual cost of such measures was an estimated $9 billion.[17]

Second, it began to search for ways to reduce its long-term direct spending obligations. Since social programs were among the most visible – thanks to the efforts of the business community to influence public opinion – they became a focus of government attention. While governments could see the inevitability of reducing such expenditures in the long term (if the country was going to rely on the private sector to drive the economy, the needs of investors would come first), cuts could not be accomplished quickly or easily. Most of the government's major social spending obligations were statutory, meaning they would require highly visible legislative action to be changed. The political risks of such a move would be high. The public in the 1970s still believed that social programs, once created, were permanent; it would be perilous for any political party to challenge that view.

Before any major steps could be taken to reduce social spending, it would become necessary to establish a new and reduced set of expectations in the public's mind regarding what the government could provide. Against this backdrop, the new "ideology of restraint" was born. Since 1975, the public has been inundated with messages about the "new reality," which demands a "more competitive" economy if Canada is to compete on world markets.

Canadians have been repeatedly told that a "leaner government" is necessary which, in turn, will require "reduced expectations" with regard to social programs. This message, continually reiterated since 1975 by the government and business with the help of the mainstream press, was designed to lay the ideological groundwork for an eventual dismantling of the welfare state.

Third, at the same time it was laying this new ideological groundwork, the government was taking immediate steps to gain control over the rate of growth of its social spending. During the 1970s, eligibility rules were tightened where possible; premiums and user fees were introduced or increased; universality was eroded in favour of means tested programs; and the cost of delivering programs was contained by wage restraints, layoffs, budget restraints and privatization. These efforts achieved their desired results. Real social expenditures rose at an annual rate of 9.5 per cent between 1960 and 1975; between 1975 and 1981, the rate of increase declined to 2.9 per cent.[18]

Fourth, to cope with its immediate fiscal needs during the 1970s, the federal government resorted to deficit financing. The full measure of the fiscal crisis can be seen in the dramatic rise of federal deficits from $145 million in 1971 to $10.3 billion in 1980.[19] While the business community railed against this trend – demanding immediate reductions in social spending – borrowing money in the short term served an important political function. It allowed the government to buy time until real cuts in spending could be rendered more acceptable.

The recession of the early 1980s exacerbated the revenue and spending patterns that contributed to the government's fiscal crisis. A significant drop in industrial activity meant a decline in government revenues from both personal and corporate taxation. Massive unemployment led to still greater demands on social programs (Unemployment Insurance in particular). High interest rates – the result of government policy – caused the cumulative public debt to soar to the point where interest payments on the debt alone accounted for an increasingly large share of the federal government's operating budget.[20]

The recession brought the political aspect of the fiscal crisis to a head and gave the business community a chance to impose its agenda on the government. Using the threat of a capital strike when Ottawa was heavily dependent upon business investment to pull the economy out of the recession, it forced the government to make deficit reduction its number one priority. The business community also ensured that the burden would not be borne by itself. It demanded, and got, the reinstatement of numerous corporate tax breaks that were unexpectedly taken away by MacEachen's 1981 budget.[21] The government's acquiescence to the demands of business was evident at the ideological level in the Prime Minister's televised talks to the nation in the fall of 1982,[22] and at the fiscal level in the Liberals' "6 & 5" program which arbitrarily capped the rate of growth of federal expenditures.[23]

Although the "need" to reduce the deficit was scarcely mentioned during the 1984 federal election campaign, it became the Conservatives' immediate priority once they were in office. While Prime Minister Brian Mulroney and his ministers engaged in heavy initial rhetoric about the necessity of reducing social spending – focusing on the principle of universality – their hypersensitivity to public opinion polls during their first term made them back off when the political heat intensified.[24] They were saved from the risks of a full-scale attack on social spending during their first term because of the high rate of economic growth. Increased revenues from this growth enabled them to meet the business community's demand for deficit reduction without undertaking a major assault on social spending. Such rates of economic growth would not be destined to last, and the tough political decisions would remain to be made.

The Political Challenges of Cutting Back

Once a government accepts the "need" to reduce social expenditures, it faces the political challenge of finding ways to do it without undermining its own prospects for re-election. Cutting back on social programs could mean disenfranchising Canadians from social benefits to which they have become accustomed and which, in many cases, they have come to view as a right.

Social programs might be likened to the lifeboats on a ship. These lifeboats have been developed to look after those who didn't contribute to the "efficient" operation of the ship. With the changes in the economy in recent years, more people have become dependent upon these lifeboats for their survival. Recently, those who "own" the fuel that propels the ship (investors) have begun telling the officers in command there is no longer enough money to meet their continuing demand for profits and the growing demand for lifeboats. Their solution to this problem is to have the government throw people out of the lifeboats.

The problem facing the government is that people in the lifeboats are not always willing to co-operate when their time comes to walk the plank. An example can be found in the groundswell of resistance that emerged when the Tories tried to partially de-index old age security in 1985.[25] The direct approach to making cuts – akin to hitting people over the head and dumping them overboard – would clearly not enhance a government's prospects for re-election. Evidence of how quickly the Conservatives learned this lesson can be found in their subsequent unwillingness (during their first term) to implement the recommendations of the Forget Commission, which called for a massive restructuring of the unemployment insurance program. While in philosophical sympathy with many of the commission's recommendations, they also recognized political suicide.

The failure of the direct approach to cutbacks did not lessen the government's "need" to reduce social expenditures. It demonstrated the need for a broader base of political support before such cuts could be implemented. Support from the business community alone would never be enough to ensure a government's re-election. The essence of the Conservatives' strategy for dealing with the fiscal crisis has been to aggressively cultivate this support from segments of the middle class.

The middle class generally consists of small-business entrepreneurs and those who derive their income from the higher levels of the wage scale: unionized blue- and white-collar workers, professionals and managers. Unfortunately, with the current attempts to down-size and privatize government services, and with the introduction of labour-saving technologies in key industrial sectors, the latter group is shrinking relative to the rest of the population. "Downward mobility" is a phrase which increasingly applies to a significant proportion of the middle class.[26]

Despite these pressures, the middle class continues to be the backbone of our liberal/democratic political system. It is the group most active in electoral politics, with the skills and resources to make itself heard through the media, and it is accustomed to a political system responsive to its needs. A government that relies on privately held capital cannot ignore the wishes of investors; a government that hopes to get re-elected cannot ignore the wishes of the middle class.

Given its strategic importance in the electoral process, the middle class will inevitably play a pivotal role in determining the outcome of *any* government strategy for resolving the fiscal crisis. It is no coincidence that since the emergence of the fiscal crisis in the mid-1970s, governments have been pursuing policies which will build support within the middle class for cuts in social spending. The middle class is being manoeuvred into a position where it will provide the government with the electoral "permission" to implement a business agenda for Canada.

The central elements of this long-term strategy have included:

- the transfer of an increasing share of the tax burden to the middle class;
- the deliberate attempt to associate this higher tax burden with the cost of maintaining social programs;
- a reduction in the benefits the middle class receives from those programs.

While these trends have been emerging since the mid-1970s, the Conservatives have greatly accelerated the rate at which they are being implemented.

Perhaps the central element in the government's long-term strategy has been the tax system. A number of trends in the field of taxation are relevant here. Over the last 30 years, the tax burden has shifted from the balance that once existed between personal and corporate taxes. In 1950, 28 per cent of government revenues came from corporate taxes, and 24 per

14   AND THE LAST SHALL BE FIRST

cent from personal income taxes. By 1984, corporations were providing only 15 per cent of revenues, while personal income tax accounted for 48 per cent.[27]

These figures don't tell the whole story. The burden of personal income tax is not borne equally by all segments of society. The poor do not have sufficient income to pay direct, personal income taxes although they do pay heavily through sales and other indirect taxes. The rich can always find ways to hide their money. Indeed, tax laws have been written largely to serve this end, and an entire industry has grown up in the last 20 years to exploit them.[28] This long-term shift from corporate to personal taxes has ultimately transferred the tax burden to the middle class.

While this trend in taxation has been occurring steadily over the last 30 years, the Tories have taken deliberate steps to accelerate it. In their 1986 budget, they announced their intention to raise personal taxes 10 times as fast as corporate taxes between 1985 and 1990 – $2.9 billion versus $295 million.[29] Michael Wilson's tax reform proposals have also reduced the marginal tax rate for the highest income earners to 29 per cent (it was 49.9 per cent in 1983, 84 per cent in 1970), and increased it for low and middle income Canadians. They have also retained "the deductibility of contributions for RRSPs and interest on funds borrowed for investments, the capital gains exemption, and the more favourable treatment of dividend income, all of which are of substantial benefit to the well-off."[30]

The government's real agenda for dealing with its fiscal crisis has been evident in the way it has justified such tax increases to the public. The problem, we are told, is too much government spending. In its attempts to locate the problem further, the Conservatives (with the vigorous support of the business community and the mainstream press) have continually pinpointed universal social programs as a prime example of unnecessary government spending: "giving money to people who don't need it."[31] The choice Canadians are being forced to make is between continually higher personal income taxes or reductions in such programs.

This attempt to link higher taxes directly with social spending has been strongly reinforced at a grassroots level by another element in the government's tax strategy – the deliberate "downloading" of the tax burden to lower levels of government. Throughout the 1980s, the federal government has used every opportunity to limit the increases in its transfer payments to the provinces.[32] Every time Ottawa caps its contributions to federal/provincial cost-shared programs (such as the Liberals' "6 & 5" program) the provinces are forced to make up the difference if services are to be maintained. Because provinces have the responsibility for delivering the programs, they get the blame if services are not maintained. Provinces are not above using the same ploy with municipalities, with the result that increased pressure is ultimately placed on municipal property taxes to provide the revenues needed to maintain existing services. The inability of municipal governments to escape this burden (by transferring the tax burden to another level of government), makes a clash of interests inevitable at their level. These are many signs it is already beginning to occur.[33]

The problem with this equation involving high taxes, the deficit, and social spending – at the national level – is that it represents a highly selective presentation of the issue. It ignores that spending on social programs as a percentage of GNP has remained relatively stable over the last 15 years; the real cause of the rising expenditures has been the cost of servicing the public debt itself: the result of revenues failing to keep pace with expenditures. Studies have consistently shown that the benefits of such tax expenditures go disproportionately to those individuals and corporations already well off.[34] By ignoring these lost revenues and treating the government's fiscal woes as a spending problem rather than a revenue problem, the government is showing its determination to resolve its fiscal crisis on the backs of those who can least afford it.

While the middle class pays more of the costs of maintaining existing social programs, other policy initiatives have helped to ensure it will benefit less. Under the guise of "fairness", the Conservatives have been seeking ways to target program benefits to those most in need. While the Prime Minister justifies this approach with rhetorical references to $500,000-a-year bank managers, the effect of this policy will be to reduce the benefits the middle class receives from social programs.

The first attempt by the Conservatives to restrict the application of programs was an attack on the principle of universality. This principle was too difficult to dislodge, at least initially. Universality has always provided the basis for middle class support for social welfare programs: a guarantee that no matter how much it paid, it would always receive some benefits. The Conservatives' retreat from their attack on universality during their first term provides a powerful demonstration of the ability of the middle class to defend its interests when it feels they are being threatened.

The government remained determined to find ways to target its programs. One method has been through tax credits. These allow the government to direct benefits toward lower income Canadians without appearing to challenge the "sacredness" of universality. The cut-off point for receiving tax credits is often set at a level which precludes much of the middle class from benefiting. While a progressive step in some respects, it also means the middle class benefits less from the programs for which it is increasingly made to pay. The Child Tax Credit instituted by the Liberals in 1978, for example, provided $200 per child to families with incomes up to $18,000. The Sales Tax Credit, introduced by the Conservatives in 1986, was available in full only to families with an annual income of less than $15,000.[35]

The government's strategy to reduce social spending has also included de-indexing the level of benefits. By increasing benefits at a rate lower than inflation, their value automatically declines over time. While forced to make a highly publicized retreat from its attempt to partially de-index old age security in 1985, the government was successful in implementing such a policy with regard to family allowances. By tying increases to the inflation rate above three percent only, the federal government saved itself an estimated $2 billion per year between 1985 and 1992.[36] This loss would be felt by all recipients, including the middle class.

The cumulative effect of these policy initiatives will be to drive a wedge between those made to pay for social programs (the middle class), and those who will continue to benefit from them (the poor, unemployed, sick, elderly – and Native people). The combination of an unsustainable tax burden accompanied by reduced benefits will lead many in the middle class to cry "Enough!" They will no longer see it as being in their economic interest to maintain such programs, and will use their skills and resources to demand reduced spending on social programs. When their demand reaches a level that will ensure re-election for the party in power, the government will be only too happy to respond.

When cuts do get made, their effect will not be felt equally by all groups. The skills and resources the middle class has to demand cutbacks will, at the same time, be used to protect those benefits it continues to enjoy. When the middle class eventually supports efforts to reduce the deficit, in other words, it will not likely be at the expense of its own RRSP deductions.[37] When push comes to shove, some spending programs will remain more "sacred" than others.

The Conservative Agenda in Action

The federal election of November 21, 1988 accomplished far more for the Conservatives than giving them a mandate to proceed with the Free Trade Agreement (FTA). The historical significance of the election was that it "flushed out" the base of electoral support the Conservatives have been needing to implement what is essentially a multinational, corporate agenda for Canada.

This corporate agenda goes beyond the mere dismantling of the welfare state. Its long-term intent is to "restructure Canadian society along continentalist and market-oriented lines"[38] and reduce the ability of the government to intervene in the economy for the benefit of all citizens.

Examples of such interventions have included: regional development subsidies; marketing boards for agricultural products; Crown corporations and state monopolies over service and resource sectors (hospitals, postal services, automobile insurance, utilities such as hydro, and minerals such as potash); pricing and export controls over energy and other resources; tariffs and taxes which discriminate in favour of Canadian or provincial companies; and income security programs which provide workers with an alternative to low-paying jobs. The FTA, over which the 1988 election was fought, represents a major step toward the implementation of this agenda because it imposes an external constraint on the federal government's ability to engage in these activities. Any government willing to enter into such an agreement has agreed to limit its ability to shape the future of Canadian society in ways other than those dictated by the market.

The 1988 election was significant as it signalled the beginning of a potential realignment of political forces within Canada – a realignment based on competing economic interests and competing visions of Canadian society. Those segments of the electorate inclined to favour a free market economy and a reduced role for government traditionally split their support between the two major political parties. In 1988, the FTA provided a catalyst for this group to coalesce around one party: the Conservatives.

While a multitude of factors undoubtedly contributed to the Conservatives' re-election,[39] it was clear that a strategically important block of voters – "highly educated, high income Canadians and the professional-managerial class"[40] lined up solidly behind the Conservatives. This segment of the electorate has the resources to compete successfully in an unfettered market economy and has the least reliance on social spending. This group also has the greatest ability to influence the political process. It is the group best able to provide the government with the "permission" to implement the corporate agenda in Canada.

The realignment of political forces in the 1988 election left the Conservatives in a stronger position to proceed with the corporate agenda than four years earlier. The election provided a base of electoral support with two characteristics: 1) It was supportive of a party committed both to deficit reduction and a reduced role for government in the economy (symbolized by the FTA); and 2) It had proven itself capable of returning a party to office with a majority. Neither the Conservatives nor the corporate sector could have asked for more.

With their political base secured, the Conservatives became more willing to implement the corporate agenda. During their first term, they were held back by their fear of negative opinion polls; with their 1988 re-election, they knew it was possible to reach historic lows in the polls and still recover in time to get re-elected with a majority. This made them more willing to withstand the short-term political heat that would accompany any specific program cuts. Examples of this new resolve were apparent in the array of initiatives undertaken during their first year back in office:

- implementation of the Free Trade Agreement with the United States, and commencement of negotiations for a North American free trade zone with Mexico;
- withdrawal of federal contributions to the Unemployment Insurance fund, leaving it financed totally by employers and workers;
- cuts to regional development programs;
- reductions in transfer payments to provinces and territories for health, welfare and education programs;
- introduction of a Goods and Services Tax;
- introduction of the "clawback" on universal social programs;
- 50% cuts to VIA rail passenger services;
- major reductions to the Canadian Broadcasting Corporation's operating budget;
- cuts to foreign aid.

The combined effect of the clawback and the Goods and Services Tax will have enormous implications for social spending in Canada. The clawback will separate even more Canadians from the social welfare benefits they have traditionally enjoyed, reducing their stake in having such programs maintained. Because the cut-off point is not designed to keep pace with the rate of inflation, it means that the proportion of the middle class that will lose its benefits will increase steadily. At the same time, the Goods and Services Tax (GST) will bring about a major increase in the tax burden on this same group. Under these conditions, the distance between those who pay and those who benefit from social programs will continue to grow.

Once universality is "broken" through the clawback and the benefits of direct social spending are confined to those "most in need," the political question facing those left to pay – the middle class – will be: How much can we afford to maintain programs that benefit 'other' people? With government continually upping the ante on the tax burden, the same forces which led the middle class to support policies of deficit reduction and an end to universality will lead them to support reduced levels of benefits to "those most in need." At that point, the real dismantling of the welfare state will begin.

At that point, Native people will once again be among the most vulnerable. As this book will show, Native people are already among the most marginalized of any group in Canada. When the competition intensifies over scarce social program resources, the extent of this marginalization will again become apparent. Racism itself may prove decisive. Is any government in Ottawa likely to defend the 35 per cent of Native spending it deems "discretionary" if it means non-Native Canadians will suffer?

Part 2:

". . . And The Last Shall Be First"

Native Policy in an Era of Cutbacks

"...And The Last Shall Be First"
Native Policy in an Era of Cutbacks

The Position of Native People in Canadian Society

Native people will inevitably be among the victims of any cuts in government spending because they are already a marginalized group in Canadian society – demographically, regionally, economically, politically and racially. As competition increases for the remaining seats in the lifeboats, these factors will ensure that Native people will be among the first to be thrown out.

A brief review of post-war history provides evidence to support this contention. The position of Native people in Canadian society can be seen by looking at when their needs were addressed in relation to the development of the welfare state. It was not until the end of the post-war boom – after the boom had peaked – that the needs of Native people began to be addressed in a systematic way by the federal government. That Ottawa's response (the 1969 White Paper)[41] was hopelessly misguided is of less importance than the timing of the initiative, after the major components of the current welfare state were already in place. It was only after the lifeboats had been established for other Canadians that consideration was given to finding room for Native people. Given that they were among the last to benefit when the welfare state was expanding, it is not unreasonable to expect they will also be among the first to suffer when the welfare state contracts. "... And the last shall be first." (Matthew 20:16)

In addition to these general considerations, there are at least three specific reasons why Native people will be among the victims of any government attempts to control or reduce social expenditures. First, monies spent on Native people come from what was once called the "social envelope"; as social spending in general comes under attack, Native people will also be vulnerable. A second factor lies with demographics: the Native population is rising at a rate far higher than the rest of the Canadian population. This means that even a continuation of existing programs would lead to increasing costs. Any government wanting to control its long-term social spending will have to find ways of reducing its existing commitments to Native people. Finally, there is racism. Native people live in the midst of a white society which, when forced to choose, will look after its own first. As a last resort, white Canadians can always call upon their government to defend their interests; Native people lack a similar option.

Since the fiscal crisis became acute in the late 1970s, the federal government has been systematically searching out ways to reduce its long-term obligations to Native people. This usually unstated objective can be discerned in practically every major policy initiative related to Native people in the last decade. Theoretically, the government has two major options for achieving this goal: 1) It can either make direct and unilateral cuts in its spending on Native programs (an approach with some political risks); or 2) It can transfer its responsibilities.

Three practical avenues are available to the Conservatives for doing the latter:

• transfer responsibilities to Native people through self-government and land claims negotiations;

• transfer responsibilities to the provinces, which the Nielsen Report implies should "normally" be providing many of the services. This strategy has been pursued implicitly through the constitutional process and self-government negotiations, and more explicitly in the negotiations to transfer program delivery responsibilities to the provinces;

• transfer responsibilities to the territorial governments. Since 1987, the Conservatives have moved rapidly to "devolve" federal responsibilities to the Government of the North West Territories.[42] A similar process has occurred in the Yukon, culminating in the signing of the Northern Energy Accords in 1988. By strengthening territorial governments, the Conservatives have met several objectives. They have dismantled their own bureaucracy, and transferred power to the North without confronting the "messy" issue of aboriginal rights.

The rest of this book addresses a more detailed examination of thrusts in Native policy to show how they are being used to achieve the long-term goal of fiscal restraint.

The Nielsen Report:
Laying the Groundwork for Cuts

While the Nielsen Report was not the first example of government attempts to control Native spending over the last decade, we should examine it first because it provides such a clear presentation of the federal government's underlying thinking about Native people and its obligations to them.

The Nielsen Report on Native programs was one of many initiated by the Tory government soon after it took office, as part of a massive review of all government spending programs. It was done by a team of "experts," most of whom had never been outside their Ottawa offices, let alone on a reserve. It contained a multitude of specific recommendations for controlling and reducing Native spending. Because of the premature release of a preliminary report – due to the courageous act of a disaffected bureaucrat – and the political heat brought to bear on the government, many of the specific recommendations were never acted upon, openly or officially.

Despite this, much of the Nielsen Report remains highly relevant. It represents the government's own "conjunctural analysis" of its relationship – and obligations – to Native people. It documents why spending restraints are necessary from the government's point of view (especially the impact of demographics), and maps out a long-term strategy for achieving them. While many of the report's recommendations were rendered politically stillborn, the structural analysis it provided of the Crown's obligations to Native people continues to be the basis for its policy initiatives.

The report begins with a review of spending levels on Native people, which it says amounted to more than $3 billion in 1984-85. It then analyses the demographic trends for the Native population as a basis for predicting government expenditures. It notes that:

• the Native population is significantly younger than the national average;

• the proportion of Indians living off-reserve has doubled from 15 per cent in 1966 to 30 per cent in 1983;

• the "working age" Native population is expected to grow at three times the national rate;

• by 1991, one in two people entering the workforce in Saskatchewan will be Native;

• fertility rates among Native people are two times the national average.[43]

The report moves on to assess the implications of these demographic trends for government expenditures. It observes that even the maintenance of existing programs (which it admits are inadequate) would lead to an increase in federal spending from $3 billion in 1985-86 to $5.05 billion in 1990-91 "as a result of demographic figures alone."[44] This projection is set against the federal government's presumed "need" to reduce spending, leading the authors to conclude that the objective should be "the reduction over time of the rapidly escalating trend in federal expenditures."[45] This, it argues, "demands not only significant adjustments to government policies and programs but also structural changes."[46]

After establishing the "need" for structural changes in the relationship between Ottawa and Native people, the report examines the patterns in federal spending to determine where such changes could be made. It telegraphs its eventual recommendations by noting: "Services have been provided far beyond the federal government's constitutional and legislative responsibility for Indians and Inuit."[47] It goes on to break down federal spending into three distinct parts:

- "only 25 per cent of federal expenditures for Indian and Native people are to meet legal obligations";

- "40 per cent pay what would normally be provincial (largely statutory) programs due to the federal responsibility for 'Indians and lands reserved for Indians' (Sec. 91.24)";

- "the remaining 35 per cent is discretionary, based on social policy decisions over time."[48]

This breakdown provides the government with the analytical framework to develop long-term strategies for reducing its spending on Native people. Translated, it clarifies for the government: 1) its minimal obligations (the 25 per cent stemming largely from treaty and land claims obligations); 2) what might be appropriate for other levels of government to pay (the 40 per cent allocated for health care, housing and education, which provinces normally provide to Canadians); and 3) what it could cut, if politically acceptable (the 35 per cent it has no legal obligation to spend).

One of the central themes of the report (second only to the reduction of expenditures) is the need for greater local control by Native people of their own affairs. While this theme is always presented in terms of its assumed advantages for Native people, Ottawa would also stand to gain significantly. To an uninformed public, a transfer of responsibility to Native people would make the government appear responsive to Native demands to "get government off our backs." It would also leave Ottawa less accountable politically and legally for the conditions of Native people – "they're managing their own affairs now."

Financially, the multi-year, block funding arrangements recommended for bands and communities would not imply any increase in expenditure. If anything, they would stabilize Ottawa's expenditures because they would prohibit "the unbridled growth of more ad hoc social policy programs"[49] which – according to the authors of the report – have contributed to the rise in spending. Greater local control would leave Native people more responsibility for their future, but would not necessarily provide them with the resources to alter – or even maintain – their current circumstances.

Some of the report's recommendations could help to further marginalize Native people. The authors push strongly for the dismantling of the Department of Indian Affairs, suggesting that "specialty services" be transferred to "specialist departments" – for example, "all economic development to be managed by Department of Regional Industrial Expansion (DRIE); employment programs by the Canadian Employment and Immigration Commission (CEIC); policing services by the Solicitor General."[50] The argument behind this recommendation is that the Department of Indian Affairs and Northern Development (DIAND) "by itself cannot be expected to have the depth of capacity to manage programs to meet all the needs of Indian and Inuit people."[51] Whatever the many benefits of dismantling DIAND, implementation of this recommendation would fragment the sources of funding to Native groups. Decisions about the allocation of funds for Native programs more likely would be made internally within departments, rather than politically around the Cabinet table.

The report also calls for a new funding structure for Native political organizations. The report suggests eliminating core funding for such organizations and giving the money "directly to bands."[52] The argument is that if the bands wanted to be politically represented, they would have the means to fund organizations that would serve their interests. The organizations would become more accountable to their constituencies than might currently be the case.

While strong rhetorical arguments could be used to justify such a move – accountability, local control, democratic principles – the implementation of such a recommendation could well lead to the "gutting" of the national political Native organizations. The majority of bands or Native communities in Canada have such pressing needs with regard to infrastructure and services, they would be under pressure to apply available funds to meet them. Political organizations in distant places might prove to be a luxury few bands and communities feel they could afford. The result would be a decline in the ability of Native people to engage in collective political action, and to defend themselves against government cutbacks. Left to act on their own, they could literally become voices crying in the wilderness within the Canadian political system.

These two potential initiatives would weaken individual bands and communities. The dismantling of DIAND would mean competition for program monies from a variety of departments on the same basis as other

28 AND THE LAST SHALL BE FIRST

Canadians. Given their remoteness from the mainstream of Canadian society – racially, geographically, demographically and culturally – Native communities would hardly be in a position to compete equally. The loss of strong political representation would reduce their capacity to push for an adequate allocation of resources and leave them even more vulnerable to government cutbacks.

Expenditure Reductions:
Nielsen by Another Name

While the Conservatives officially disassociated themselves from the controversial recommendations of the Nielsen Report when it was prematurely leaked in 1985, the record shows they have used their term in office to achieve major cuts in Native spending. Before discussing how the Conservatives achieved this, it is best to get a full measure of the reductions that have occurred. While the government claims that overall DIAND spending has increased significantly (42 per cent) during its first term in office,[53] a closer examination of the data reveals a different – and darker – story.

In capital expenditures – housing and other forms of community infrastructure – the government's estimates show an increase in DIAND spending by 38.9 per cent from 1984-85 to 1988-89. Two factors need to be taken into account before the real impact of these "increases" can be measured. First, inflation rose 22 per cent during the same period, making the value of the dollars significantly less. Second, the Native population served by these expenditures increased dramatically (24 per cent) during the same period, meaning the funds had to be spread among more people. When inflation and population growth were taken into account, the result was a decline in capital expenditures by 14.8 per cent over four years.[54]

The same story exists with non-capital expenditures – programs and services. While outwardly the spending by DIAND increased by 31.9 per cent over four years, when inflation and population growth were factored in, the effect was a 10.2 per cent decrease in the value of those expenditures for Native people. Taken together, "the net result (has been) a significant decline in financial resources" available to Native people since the Conservatives took office in 1984.[55]

The prescriptions for cutbacks outlined in the Nielsen Report have not been used by the Conservatives to achieve these reductions. Instead, they have employed a combination of other direct and indirect methods, including:

1. *Unilateral Cuts*: The Conservatives have not been averse to making direct cuts in program expenditures. In the 1988-89 fiscal year, spending on self-government was reduced 17 per cent (from $13.5 million to $11.2 million); on comprehensive claims by 6.2 per cent (from $78.2 million to $73.3 million); on economic development by 19.2 per cent (from $82.5 million to $66.6 million); and on lands, reserves & trusts by 14.7 per cent (from $48.1 million to $41.1 million) – all in relation to the previous fiscal year. In the previous two years, DIAND funds for human resource development were reduced by 50 per cent and funds for renewable resource development were reduced from $30 million to $4 million.[56]

2. *Not Keeping Pace With Inflation*: This represents the "backdoor" approach to expenditure reduction. While the figures on the books don't indicate any cutbacks, the lack of an inflationary increase means the recipients receive less each year. Funding for Native organizations has remained static since the Conservatives took office. With inflation running at an average of 5.3 per cent annually during the same period, this represents a 21.2 per cent cut in operating budgets during the Conservatives' first term. The budget for Native housing, while keeping pace with inflation, has not kept up with the rise in construction costs, resulting in less money for housing starts in Native communities.

3. *Devolution*: The Mulroney government has been moving rapidly to dismantle its own bureaucracy and to transfer program and administrative responsibilities to Native people. When such transfers occur, the accompanying financial resources do not take into account the hidden costs of administration – capital costs such as buildings and rent. They also don't take into account the range of technical and professional supports traditionally provided at no cost to DIAND by other government departments: legal services by the Department of Justice, and property management by the Department of Public Works. Every time DIAND transfers responsibilities to a Native group, the government no longer has to provide such "hidden" services, and can save itself money. Native people are left to administer the same range of responsibilities, without access to a similar array of resources.

4. *Restricting the Interpretation of Rights*: The Conservatives have shown a propensity for unilaterally reinterpreting historic rights if it serves their cost reduction purposes. The most blatant example has been education for status Indians. As more young people have sought opportunities for post-secondary education, the Conservatives have restricted access to these benefits. In 1987, Minister of Indian and Northern Affairs Bill McKnight announced major revisions in the federal policy, including a "capping" of funds, and the introduction of a system for "prioritizing" Native students.

5. *Cutting Funds for Lobbying*: "Stunned." That was the word used by Georges Erasmus, National Chief of the Assembly of First Nations, to describe his reaction to the cutbacks introduced by Michael Wilson in the February, 1990 budget. It was a word which aptly described the feelings of many others in the Native community.

The measures which provoked this reaction included the following:
- the elimination of core funding for the Assembly of First Nations, as well as for twenty-seven regional tribal councils;
- a 15% reduction in core funding for seven other First Nations organizations, as well as the Inuit Tapirisat of Canada;
- the complete elimination of the Native Communications Program, which sustained 15 Native language newspapers across Canada;
- a 16% reduction in funding for the Native Broadcast Access Program which supports television and radio broadcasting in remote parts of the country;
- a reduction of $1.2 million in the budget for Native friendship centres;
- a 5% cap on spending increases for the next two years on programs covering self-government, economic development, lands and trusts, capital spending, community services, band management and language.

These sweeping measures were striking for a variety of reasons:

First, they suggest that the era of restraint is over, and that the era of actual reduction has begun. Prior to this budget, the federal government relied heavily on the "back door" approach to fiscal restraint, with the primary goal of slowing the rate of growth in Native expenditures. By not increasing aboriginal organizations' budgets at the full rate of inflation, for example, Ottawa was able to maintain the public appearance of support, at the same time eroding the organizations' actual effectiveness.

With the 1990 budget, the need to keep up such appearances has obviously come to an end. The elimination of core funding to the Assembly of First Nations (AFN) in particular represents an act of astonishing boldness by the Conservatives. Without such funds, the AFN will be entirely dependent upon short-term "project" funds, which will give the government almost complete control over its activities. If the Conservatives can gut the strongest and most effective Native organization in the country and come out unscathed, they will have little to fear in confronting other areas of Native spending in a similar fashion in the years ahead.

The boldness of the budget measures provides yet another indication of the attitudinal change that has occurred within the Conservative government since it was re-elected in 1988. No longer phobic about the potential loss of popularity, the Prime Minister now appears almost smug in his indifference to his government's low standing in the public opinion polls. This willingness to sustain low popularity accounts for their current willingness to attack Native spending in such a high profile manner.

It is all important to note how strategically planned these cuts were. Native programs were not the unintended victims in a general process of cutbacks; nor were all Native programs equally affected. Rather, they were singled out in a detailed and deliberate way. The most vocal groups – the AFN, James Bay Cree, Nisga'a, Gitksan Wet'suwet'en – lost 100 per cent of their core funding. Given the fact that the overall amount saved will be inconsequential in terms of deficit reduction (the alleged goal), one can only conclude that these cuts were carried out largely for political reasons – as "surgical strikes" to eliminate those with the greatest potential to oppose the government/corporate agenda.

On a broader note, the attack on the AFN must also be seen as an attempt by the government to undermine the coalition-building occurring among popular sector groups over the last decade. During the 1980s, representatives of labour unions, churches, womens' groups, Native and anti-poverty organizations began to get increasingly familiar with and involved in each other's issues and struggles. It was in the free trade debate during the 1988 election that these working relations began to acquire an ongoing and formal structure – principally, through the Pro-Canada Network. The AFN, under the leadership of Georges Erasmus, was a significant participant in this process.

While this national popular sector coalition has been largely ignored by the mainstream press and most established politicians, the government is obviously aware of its presence and its potential to act as an "extra-parliamentary opposition" to the government/corporate agenda. It is no coincidence that in its 1990 budget, the two groups most affected by spending cuts were aboriginal people and women. Of the various sectors represented in coalitions, these were most dependent upon government funds for their existence (labour and churches are relatively self-financing, by comparison). The cuts in funding to the AFN and to womens' centres across the country should be seen as a pre-emptive strike by the Tories against these emerging popular sector coalitions.

Self-Government:
The Real Buffalo Jump of the 1990s?

In recent years, the diverse aspirations of Native people throughout Canada have been expressed in a single phrase: "self-government." While self-government could take a multitude of forms – as many as there are nations or communities – the phrase has emerged as the single most effective way for aboriginal people to communicate their vision of a hopeful future within Confederation.

From the government's point of view, self-government represents something else entirely: an historic opportunity to restructure its legal, political and fiscal relations with Native people. For a government faced with a fiscal crisis, and desperately seeking ways to reduce its long-term responsibilities for Native people, the Native quest for self-government represents a gift. By harnessing the rhetoric associated with self-government and local control, the government has been trying to legitimize actions to further its agenda of "getting out of the Native business."

Whatever its form, Native self-government will require three things: 1) a recognition by the government of Native authority in specific areas of jurisdiction; 2) a recognized structure for exercising that authority; and 3) the economic resources to make that structure work.

In terms of Native jurisdiction, the federal government has been quite willing to consider the transfer of certain responsibilities to Native bands and tribal councils. At the same time, it has been determined to control the process by which such transfers take place to ensure its objectives will be realized.

Ottawa controls the self-government process by denying Native people any legal or constitutional right to self-government. Such a right would enable Native people to assert their own jurisdiction, with the potential backing of the courts, and implications – political and financial – for the federal and provincial governments. By not recognizing the right, Native people are left to take what is offered, when the government chooses to offer it.

The government has denied Native people the right to self-government on all three fronts where the issue has arisen in the 1980s. First, at the constitutional level, it has rejected any open-ended recognition of a right to self-government and offered only a watered-down version – a right to negotiate self-government. Even this offer must remain suspect, because it was made with the knowledge that it would lack the support of both the Native groups and the provinces (although for different reasons). Second, in land claims negotiations, Ottawa has left the door open for the negotiation of self-government in the Dene/Métis and Yukon claims, but only on condition that such rights would not receive the same constitutional protection accorded the rest of the settlements. The basic fear underlying this "policy of denial" is that constitutional recognition of an aboriginal right to self-government in any context would establish a legal precedent that could be used by other Native groups across Canada to assert their self-government agendas.

Third, the government's self-government policy reflects this strategy. Its intention is to proceed with the development of self-government pending the constitutional recognition of such a right. While the policy statements extol the need for "flexibility" in the timing and substance of self-government negotiations (letting bands "take the initiative – when they are ready"), the effect of the policy is to limit the parameters of what can be negotiated. Bands that want to receive funds to develop plans for self-government must first accept those parameters. The result will be a limited form of self-government based on a municipal model, with responsibilities "delegated" to bands by the federal government. While the result offers some advantages to Native communities, they can still only exercise jurisdiction in those areas which Ottawa permits. Ottawa retains the right to decide which bands are at a sufficiently "advanced" stage to be "ready" for even this limited form of self-government.

As mentioned earlier, this model of local control has many benefits for the federal government. Legally, it allows Ottawa complete control over what powers are transferred to Native people – and when. Politically and legally, it leaves Ottawa with less responsibility for what happens in Native communities. Financially, the new Alternative Funding Arrangements (AFA) – essentially, block funding – will permit more stable, hence predictable, federal spending.

Any self-government arrangement will require sufficient resources to be successful. Those resources can only come from two sources: 1) transfer payments from Ottawa; and/or 2) greater access to lands and resources in their traditional territories. In the first case, Ottawa has made it clear that its proposed Alternate Funding Arrangements will not lead to any increase in funding. They simply allow Native communities more control over the funds they are currently receiving. Given the conditions in most Native communities, Native people will be left with little more than the responsibility for administering their own poverty.

In the absence of any increase in federal transfer payments, Native communities will require an increased land and resource base if self-government is to succeed. This will not be easy to acquire. The existing land and resource base of Native people is already under growing pressure from outside users. The 1980s have witnessed an increasing number of serious, sometimes violent, conflicts between Native and non-native resource users throughout Canada, involving the Micmacs in Nova Scotia and Restigouche; the Algonquin of Barrier Lake; the Bear Island band in Temagami; the White Dog and Grassy Narrows bands in northwestern Ontario; the Cree of Lubicon Lake, the Haida and Gitksan Wet'suwet'en of British Columbia. In each case, attempts by Native groups to assert even their existing rights to lands and resources have met increasing resistance from well-organized commercial and industrial interests.[57] Any attempt to expand Native access to, or control over, these resources – fish, game, forests, wild rice, oil, gas or minerals – can expect to meet fierce resistance from non-native interests.

To appreciate the challenge aboriginal people face in expanding their land base, consider what has happened to lands that are already supposed to be theirs. After the treaties were signed on the Prairies 100 years ago, the federal government admittedly failed to provide the reserve lands it had promised. When control over the land was transferred to the Provinces of Saskatchewan and Alberta in 1930, it was on the condition that unoccupied Crown land would eventually be made available to the federal government to allow it to meet these obligations. Attempts to negotiate a resolution of these so-called "land entitlement" claims in recent years have been undermined not only by federal/provincial infighting about who should pay, but also by organized resistance from rural municipalities which fear the loss to their tax base of lands withdrawn for reserve purposes.[58] Opposition to an expanded Native land base could as easily come from the grassroots as from specialized corporate interests.

Who will Native communities look to for assistance in their struggle for a greater land or resource base? The federal government has shown little interest in asserting Native rights to resources beyond the interests of non-natives (the Lubicon experience is the most glaring illustration). Ottawa has political and financial reasons for its inactivity. Politically, an aggressive defense of Native interests, at the expense of competing white interests, could alienate potential voters. Financially, Ottawa also has responsibility for compensating the provinces for any lands and resources that might be removed from provincial jurisdiction for the benefit of Native people. The price B.C. Premier Bill Vander Zalm recently extracted from Ottawa for the creation of a national park on South Moresby – an estimated $106 million[59] – indicates the price Ottawa will be made to pay for the alienation of any resource-rich provincial lands. Given its determination to limit expenditures, and the unimportance of Native people electorally, can Ottawa be expected to go to the wall for Native people in their quest for an expanded resource base to adequately finance self-government?

Provincial governments will feel they have nothing to gain, and much to lose, by allowing Native people increased access to lands and resources. The same lands and resources provide the provinces with their most important independent source of revenue. To relinquish any lands, and the benefits that flow from them in taxes and royalties, would cause their own revenue base to shrink – not an attractive option for any government struggling to cope with its own fiscal crisis.

Provincial governments are also the agents of local interests, to a greater degree than the federal government. This means they are responsive to the needs and demands of their own resource industries and/or rural municipalities. If constraints are imposed on these groups in reduced access to land and resources, they will not likely be initiated by provincial governments. The only way they would consider making land available to Native people is if the federal government agreed to provide adequate compensation for the loss. Is Ottawa likely to hand over large amounts of money to the provinces when its own fiscal house is in such disorder? Given the competition over increasingly scarce resources, and the fiscal needs of most provincial governments, the underlying conflict of interest between Native people and the provinces is probably more relevant today than it was when the BNA Act was drawn up in 1867. Without broad public support, this is unlikely to change.

The Constitutional Process:
"Embroiling the Provinces"

If the success of a lobbying effort is measured by the extent to which an issue gains acceptance on the national political agenda, the early 1980s may be looked upon as the heyday of Native rights activism in Canada in the 20th century. Not only did Native people secure a place for themselves in the new Canadian Constitution, they also succeeded in getting the First Ministers of Canada to meet with them for eight days (over four years) to discuss the details of their rights – on live, nation-wide television. For a group that constitutes approximately three per cent of the Canadian population, this represents no small achievement.

Native people were not the only ones who came to the constitutional talks with an agenda. The federal government, mindful of its long-term financial responsibilities, looked upon the process as an historic opportunity to get the provinces involved in Native issues – something the provinces have traditionally been loath to do.

Under the BNA Act, the federal government was given exclusive responsibility for "Indians and lands reserved for Indians." This was later interpreted by the courts to include Inuit, but until 1982, the Métis and non-status Indians had no constitutional status. The allocation was made on the basis of two assumptions. First, the provinces couldn't be trusted to protect aboriginal rights because the exercise of such rights would conflict with provincial jurisdiction over lands and resources. Second, it was assumed that Native people were destined to assimilate anyway, so the burden of exclusive responsibility would only be temporary. While the first of these assumptions has stood the test of time, the second has not.

For the next 100 years, the provinces continued to view aboriginal rights as a potential threat to their control over lands and resources. Since entering Confederation in 1871, for example, B.C. has refused to acknowledge the existence of aboriginal rights. Until the new Constitution was drafted, the provinces generally wanted nothing to do with such rights, and were only too happy to leave the problem to the federal government. To the extent aboriginal rights were recognized by the provinces, they were viewed in the narrowest possible terms, and always with the proviso that Ottawa pick up the tab.

The federal government took the initiative to get aboriginal rights on the constitutional reform agenda. The timing of its initiative again revealed its priorities. When the first round of talks aimed at constitutional renewal took place under Prime Minister Pierre Trudeau in the late 1960s and early 1970s, no serious consideration was given to the inclusion of aboriginal rights. (This reflected the fact that there were no national Native organizations able to press the issue.) As its own fiscal crisis deepened by the late 1970s, and the implications of its constitutional responsibilities to Native people became increasingly apparent, Ottawa began to develop its own reasons for including aboriginal rights on the agenda for constitutional reform.

Given the clarity of the BNA Act with regard to federal responsibility for Native people and that most provinces were experiencing a fiscal crisis, there was no reason for Ottawa to assume the provinces would volunteer to pick up costs for the provision of services to Native people. By placing aboriginal rights on the constitutional agenda, the federal government achieved something that it hoped might gradually lead to the realization of that goal: it got the provinces to discuss aboriginal rights and issues.

The enticement used by the federal government to get the provinces to the table was the provision that the latter would retain a veto over any definition of aboriginal rights. The provinces' acceptance of this arrangement signified an historic shift in their constitutional relationship with Native people. Whereas they had no previous constitutional role and had to be dragged into any discussion of Native rights, the new Constitution gave them control over what those rights might be. Instead of reacting to threats against their jurisdiction, the new Constitution gave the provinces the ability to prevent such threats from ever arising.

Ottawa's strategy for the constitutional process was outlined in an internal memo leaked prior to the first conference in 1982. It consisted of two parts: 1) reducing Native expectations; 2) embroiling the provincial governments in the process of discussion and perhaps negotiation.

"Reducing Native expectations" was a polite way of saying Ottawa had no intention of recognizing an expanded array of constitutional rights for Native people. "Embroiling" the provinces, on the other hand, served a number of functions. First, it would help to ensure that no major breakthroughs would occur for Native people because there would always be enough provinces willing to exercise their veto. Second, Ottawa hoped that by getting the provinces involved in a discussion of Native problems, they couldn't leave the table without agreeing to share some of the responsibility for solving them. In short, Ottawa was more interested in using the constitutional process to spread its own responsibilities around than in expanding the recognition of aboriginal rights.

The failure of the subsequent First Ministers' Conferences to achieve anything substantive demonstrates the lack of commitment by all governments in Canada to a meaningful definition of aboriginal rights. It appeared that the federal and provincial governments had achieved their objectives before the conferences even began.

Ottawa succeeded by getting the provinces to talk about Native issues. While it had no power to force the provinces beyond that point, Ottawa hoped in the long term that these discussions would lead to greater provincial involvement in Native issues, and ultimately to a sharing of responsibility for solving them. Many provinces did express a willingness to discuss "improved services" to Native people as an alternative to the entrenchment of any new, undefined, constitutional right. While this approach was scorned by Native leaders, it must have brought a smile to the faces of federal strategists.

The provinces got what they wanted in an unprecedented degree of control over how aboriginal rights would be defined – if they would be defined – with no formal strings of responsibility attached. The premiers paid their dues by showing up for the required conferences, but their hearts – more accurately, their interests – weren't in it. Their most persistent defence against the recognition of any new aboriginal rights was that the implications of such rights would not be known in advance. The credibility of this argument was shattered shortly afterwards when the same premiers accepted the Meech Lake Accord, with its recognition of Quebec as a "distinct society" – a term left to the courts to interpret.[60] Even when offered a watered-down amendment that would have entrenched only the right of Native people to negotiate self-government, leaving the provinces' veto power intact, they still refused.

It was clear that continual requests by the premiers for "greater clarification" were little more than a stalling tactic, and they eventually succeeded in running out of time. While forced to take their lumps from angry Native leaders on live TV, it was a small price to pay for what had been gained. With their constitutional obligations behind them (in terms of attending conferences), few will likely return to do it again.

If the players in the constitutional reform process were given scores, they would be: Provinces 3; Ottawa 1; Native people 0.

Specific Claims:
What Price, Honour?

The federal government's specific claims policy can be likened to the safety chain on the inside of an apartment door: its purpose is to limit entry. In the context of specific claims, the "door" symbolizes the bureaucratic point of entry that the government has established to enable Native people to seek redress for past wrongs; the "chain" is the mechanism or policy the government uses to limit the number of people who actually get through. In the years since the Conservatives have come to power, this "door" has been steadily closing.

Specific claims are those which relate to the government's improper administration of Indian land and other assets, and to the (non)fulfilment of Indian treaties. (Comprehensive claims, by comparison, involve the negotiation of treaties where none have yet been signed). In practice, specific claims generally involve cases in which the government has failed to provide lands it once promised, or it has mismanaged lands and assets for which it was responsible (by allowing land to be sold or taken illegally, or mismanaging band funds and assets).[61]

While the history of Native grievances against the government is as long as the country's own history, contemporary policy for dealing with such matters is a mere 20 years old. When the Trudeau government brought out its now infamous White Paper on Indian Policy in 1969, its goal was to end the special legal and constitutional status that, in its words, had "kept the Indian apart from and behind other Canadians."[62] As part of its strategy, it attempted to diminish the value assigned to treaties, portraying them as legal relics which were "irrelevant in the light of a rapidly changing world." It argued that treaties contained only "limited and minimal promises," most of which had now been fulfilled, and that their significance in meeting the needs of Native people "had always been limited, and would continue to decline." It went on to urge that "further study and research" should be done by a government appointed Commissioner [63] to identify any outstanding grievances, so these could be dealt with "as soon as possible." Otherwise, the principal reason for reviewing treaties was "to see how they [could] be equitably ended."[64]

The release of the 1969 White Paper was the formative event in the contemporary era of Native politics. The duplicity shown by government politicians and bureaucrats in the process of consultation preceding the

White Paper's release [65] provoked deep anger in Native communities across the country, anger which was subsequently directed into new levels of political activity and organization. The government seriously underestimated the value Indians continued to place on their treaties. As experience would soon show, it also greatly overestimated the extent to which its own obligations had been met.

The vociferous reaction of the Native community to the 1969 White Paper, combined with the surprisingly successful assertion of Native rights in the courts in the early 1970s,[66] forced the Trudeau government to rethink its whole approach to Native rights. No longer able to ignore the issue, either politically or legally, it opted for a change in strategy. In August of 1973, it brought out a new policy which called for the resolution of outstanding claims and grievances through a process of negotiation.

In its 1973 policy statement the government first established the administrative distinction between specific and comprehensive claims. While much of the statement dealt with the government's newfound willingness to negotiate the rights of Native people who had never signed treaties with the Crown (comprehensive claims), it also reaffirmed its intention to "honour lawful obligations" (specific claims). This, it said, would "remain [sic] the basis of Government policy."[67]

The bureaucratic mechanism established to administer this new policy was the Office of Native Claims (ONC), situated within DIAND.[68] This office was to provide the "point of entry" for Native people seeking redress for past wrongs committed against them by the Crown. The process established for dealing with outstanding grievances was as follows:

First, a claim, backed by historical research, would be submitted to ONC for consideration. Second, the claim along with its supporting documentation would be reviewed by ONC officials. Using its own research an agreement on the facts would be reached between the two parties. Third, the claim would be handed over to the Department of Justice, which would decide if a "lawful obligation" existed. If the claim was deemed "valid," the government would agree to enter into negotiations to fulfil its obligations. If not, the claim would be rejected, and the matter would end.

While the establishment of a process for dealing with their grievances was a significant step for Native people, the subsequent operation of this process rendered it a much smaller step than had been hoped.

For one thing, the establishment of ONC demonstrated to the government how badly it underestimated the potential grievances against itself. In the 1969 White Paper, it implied that virtually all of its past promises were kept ". . . except in respect of the Indians of the Northwest Territories and a few bands in the northern parts of the Prairie Provinces."[69] The assumption that specific claims would consist of little more than a "mopping up" operation in the remote regions of the country did not hold true once a single, identifiable forum (ONC) was provided to express outstanding grievances. By 1985, DIAND was predicting it would have to deal with up to 2,500 "specific" claims.[70]

The process established for dealing with such claims was frustratingly slow. The legal complexity of the issues involved, the resistance of the Department of Justice to setting legal precedents, the unexpectedly large number of claims submitted, and the limited staff resources available to ONC – all combined to move the settlement process at a glacial-like pace. Out of 242 claims submitted by 1980, only eight (3.3 per cent) were settled. At such a rate, it is estimated that it could take 40 years to settle the claims DIAND currently expects to receive.[71]

The difficulties with the claims resolution process go beyond its pace. Native groups have argued from the outset that structural factors inherent in the process also block a just resolution of their claims. They point out that the requirement that claims be based on the narrowly defined notion of "lawful obligations" means claims based on broader "principles of fairness and equity" – which take into account the "complex historical and moral issues involved" in Native/government relations – are excluded from consideration.[72] The strict burden of proof required to demonstrate the existence of a "lawful obligation" works to the disadvantage of Native groups because of the passage of time, and the lack of documentary evidence to reflect the Native experience. In its own circulars, ONC freely admits that "notions of morality, fairness, and unconscionable dealings [do] not enter into..." the consideration of what constitutes a "valid" claim.[73]

Even within the context of claims which meet the "lawful obligations" criteria, the federal government retains disproportionate control over both the process and its outcome. The determination of whether a "lawful obligation" exists is made internally by the government, often by a single lawyer from the Department of Justice. The government is in the enviable position of being its own judge, as well as the defendant – it gets to decide which claims against itself are valid, and which will be accepted for negotiation.[74] This fundamental conflict of interest is compounded by the fact that the federal government also has a constitutional responsibility to defend the interests of aboriginal people, an obligation recently reinforced by the courts.[75] By rights, the government has an obligation to be the prosecutor as well.

If the government chooses to reject a claim, no written reasons have to be provided to the claimant group. The critical role played by individual lawyers from the Department of Justice inevitably leads to inconsistencies in the determination of what constitutes a "lawful obligation," yet there are few opportunities to review these legal opinions.[76] The only way claimant groups can challenge the government's legal opinion is by going to court – not a readily available option for many poverty-stricken bands, especially when it means opposing a government with virtually unlimited legal and financial resources to defend itself.

Even when a claim is deemed "valid" by the government's narrow and legalistic terms, it does not mean negotiations will automatically occur. Not only is the government willing to deliberately ignore "notions of morality [and] fairness" in its consideration of grievances, but it is not above letting the potential cost of a settlement influence its decision to negotiate. In cases where the Department of Justice confirms that a "lawful obligation" exists, the Office of Native Claims may still refuse to enter into negotiations if the cost of a settlement has the potential to overwhelm ONC's limited budget. Bands with such legally valid but expensive claims are not offered redress by the government through negotiations, as the policy would imply. They are left to go to court because the government is not willing to allocate the funds necessary to redress the grievance – unless forced by the courts.

These criticisms were well documented by Native groups after only a few years of the policy's application. When the Trudeau government returned to power in 1980, progress on both comprehensive and specific claims was so slow that an internal review of the 1973 policy was conducted. The new policy statements that emerged from this review – *In All Fairness* in 1981, dealing with comprehensive claims, and *Outstanding Business* in 1982, dealing with specific claims – were major disappointments. Rather than initiating major changes to the previous policy, they elaborated on the assumptions that had been operative since 1973, and clarified the limits of what the government was willing to negotiate. The lack of significant change in the policy was reflected in the slow pace at which claims continued to be settled: by 1986, only 27 out of 346 submitted claims (7.8 per cent) had reached a negotiated resolution.[77]

When the Conservatives came to power in 1984, an initial flurry of attention was paid to comprehensive claims policy, including the creation of a high profile task force, which led to the eventual release of a new policy in 1986. Specific claims, by comparison, were allowed to languish. Since the Conservatives have come to power, the specific claims process has suffered from an increasing degree of political and bureaucratic neglect. The Crown's commitment to "honouring its lawful obligations," in other words, has been in steady decline.

This reduced commitment to the resolution of grievances can be seen on a number of fronts:

Bureaucratically, the status of the Office of Native Claims has been downgraded within the structure of the Department of Indian Affairs since the Conservatives took office. ONC once had its own assistant deputy minister, but is now headed by a director, a position two rungs lower on the bureaucratic ladder. There has also been a revolving door at this position, with four different directors filling the post in the last five years. When the Conservatives came to power, four full-time negotiators were working on specific claims; two have since departed and not been replaced, despite the growing backlog of claims. These trends have had a serious effect on the morale of those who have remained, as well as on ONC's overall ability to "deliver the goods." As more good people depart to other bureaucratic locales where the action – and commitment – is greater (self-government), the specific claims office has become even more of a "bureaucratic backwater" than before.

Politically, the Conservatives have also demonstrated less commitment to the resolution of Native grievances. The most glaring example has been the so-called "land entitlement" claims on the Prairies. As mentioned previously, these claims exist because the Crown failed to provide Indians with all the land originally promised in the treaties 100 years ago. The federal government has never questioned the validity of these claims. Indeed, when it transferred control of the land to the three prairie provinces in 1930, it made it clear that "unoccupied Crown land" would eventually have to be made available to meet outstanding treaty obligations.

If the facts behind these "entitlement claims" have never been in question, the method for solving them has long remained contentious. Two questions are at the heart of the dispute:

How should the amount of land owed to the Indians now be calculated? Traditionally, reserve lands were calculated on the basis of one square mile per family of five. But if all the land wasn't provided at the time of the reserve's first survey, which population figures should be used to calculate the shortfall? The population at the time the treaty was signed? When the land was first selected? When the reserve was first surveyed? Or should the population figures be taken from today, when the government is finally fulfilling its obligations?

The question of which formula should be used remained unresolved until the mid-1970s, when an effort was made to break the deadlock. In 1977, a tripartite agreement was reached in Saskatchewan involving Ottawa, the Saskatchewan government, and the Federation of Saskatchewan Indian Nations (FSIN). This agreement, dubbed the "Saskatchewan Formula," agreed to calculate reserve lands on the basis of the population figures on December 31, 1976. For Saskatchewan Indians, it would have increased their land base by up to 1.3 million acres.

While this agreement was never given legislative force, it did provide a basis for settling at least two northern claims,[78] and the intent was to use it for more. But time passed, and as governments changed at the federal and provincial levels, so did the political commitment to complete the process of land entitlement. When Grant Devine's Conservative government took office in Saskatchewan in 1984, it announced it would no longer adhere to the 1976 formula to calculate the amount of land for entitlements, and would instead use population figures from the time the treaties were first signed. (This would have reduced the amount of new lands available for Reserves to 155,000 acres). While federal Conservatives initially condemned the province's stance, arguing that the 1977 Agreement was still binding, by 1987 they too had changed their minds and decided to walk away from their previous commitment. A leaked federal government document from January 1988 revealed their new strategy: it said that the government now wished "to proceed pragmatically (no announcement) with selected negotiations based on land entitlements to date of first survey. (Not prepared to go further unless forced by courts eventually)."[79] In other words, they would negotiate with any Band that was willing to accept the more restrictive formula, and if the Indians wanted more, they would have to take the government to court – at their own expense.

It was political pressure, not court action, that eventually moved the issue ahead. In response to growing Native militancy – made visible by demonstrations and hunger strikes across the country in protest against cuts in post-secondary education funding – Ottawa appointed a "Treaty Commissioner" in September 1989 to come up with ways to deal with the fallout from education cuts, and to resolve the land entitlement issue as well. The Commissioner, Cliff Wright, submitted his report to the Minister of Indian Affairs in May 1990. It called for a total of 841,000 acres of land to be transferred to the 27 bands that had outstanding claims, and for $74.3 Million to be provided in compensation. Six months later, the federal government announced that the "Wright Formula" would indeed be an acceptable basis for settling outstanding claims.

The acceptance by Ottawa of this formula, however, does not guarantee that settlements will be reached. The second unanswered question that has long prevented the land entitlement claims from being settled is: *Who will pay for the land?* When Ottawa transferred the land to the prairie provinces in 1930, it was on the condition that they would make available the lands needed to complete the Reserves promised in the treaties. But the transfer agreement did not specify whether the federal government would have to compensate the provinces for such lands, or whether they would be handed over free of charge upon request. When the time came, the provinces naturally argued that Ottawa had an obligation to provide compensation for any lands removed from their jurisdiction. Ottawa, on the other hand, argued that no such obligation was implied in the terms of the transfer agreement. The result, not surprisingly, has been a stalemate which has provided both governments with a convenient justification for decades of inaction.

Even after the specific claims process was established in 1973, and the "Saskatchewan Formula" was introduced in 1977, the jurisdictional dispute over who should pay continued to be the most persistent barrier to any claims settlements. During the 1980s, the rural municipalities also became involved: they argued that the transfer of municipal lands to reserve status was a serious threat to their tax base, and that they too should be compensated by Ottawa for any losses. Ottawa has steadfastly refused to meet this demand, arguing that the municipalities have been collecting taxes for decades on lands which should not have been included on their tax rolls. With all levels of government trying to avoid being stuck with the tab, and neither Ottawa nor the provinces wanting to lose the all-important support of white, rural voters, a quick resolution of these outstanding claims is far from guaranteed.

Despite its recent commitment, therefore, the willingness of the federal government to "honor its outstanding obligations" still waits to be proven.

Comprehensive Claims:
One Step Forward, Two Steps Back

Much has happened on the comprehensive claims front since the Conservatives took office in 1984 – far more than would have been predicted at the outset of their term. A major review of claims policy was undertaken, culminating in the landmark Coolican Report of 1986, and by the fall of 1989 three agreements-in-principle were signed involving the largest claims in the country: the Dene/Métis, Yukon Indians, and the Inuit of the Eastern Arctic. After a decade of stalled talks under the Trudeau Liberals, these achievements appeared to signify undeniable progress.

To assess the significance of these events, it is necessary to go back to the origins of the process itself and be reminded of what Native groups originally sought to achieve through their land claims negotiations. The comprehensive claims process was born in an era when Native people, particularly in northern regions, were threatened with sudden, uncontrolled development pressures. Faced with the prospect of having their lands and communities irreparably changed by outside forces, with no guaranteed benefits in return, Native people began to organize to assert their rights.

The government's first response was to deny they had any rights. On the basis of this assumption, which it was confident the courts would support, Ottawa backed industry's plans as if Native people didn't exist. When public sympathy for the Native position began to emerge, the government modified its position slightly and expressed a willingness to discuss the concerns of Native people, if only for appearances. Its motives remained entirely political; assuming it still held all the legal cards, it felt under no obligation to respond to Native demands.

Ottawa's strategy was thoroughly undermined when the Supreme Court of Canada rendered its historic Calder decision in January, 1973. In this decision, the Court ruled unanimously that aboriginal people who had never signed treaties could, in theory, retain aboriginal title to the lands they traditionally used and occupied. Such a right could be extinguished only if it had been surrendered in a treaty or superseded by other laws passed by the Crown.

This decision had momentous implications for the struggles occurring in the North. Because the majority of Native people north of the 60th parallel had never signed treaties (the Dene signed Treaties 8 and 11, but were contesting them with initial success in the courts), it meant that Inuit, Dene, and Yukon Indians still potentially retained a legal right to lands covering one-third of Canada. The possible existence of such rights in the hands of Native people injected new and unexpected uncertainties into the development process. It meant Native people had a legal basis from which to challenge the government's jurisdiction over the lands in the North and, by extension, the activities of developers. That the courts had failed to clarify what specific rights were associated with aboriginal title only increased the uncertainty for both government and industry.

Not surprisingly, Native groups in the North gained enormous political leverage from the Calder decision. Industry was moving ahead rapidly with plans for mega-project developments, and Ottawa was providing logistical, financial and political support. The legal wild card dealt to Native people by the courts threw the whole question of authority over the North into the air. Suddenly, the government had its own reasons for wanting to talk.

Six months after the Supreme Court ruling, the Liberal government brought out a new policy for dealing with the rights of aboriginal people who had never signed treaties. While it confirmed the government's newfound willingness to talk, it also demonstrated Ottawa's determination to control the outcome of any negotiations. The policy, announced on August 3, 1973, was not intended to facilitate any sharing of power with Native people, particularly over development. Instead, it established a process for negotiations that would culminate in the payment of large amounts of cash to Native people in exchange for the extinguishment of whatever aboriginal rights they might possess. This offer represented little more than an updated version of the treaties signed 100 years ago on the Prairies; it was an approach designed to buy Native people off and to eliminate their ability to intrude on the decision-making process, especially as it related to impending resource development in their homelands.

Cognizant, perhaps, of the experience of other Native people in the South who had been "bought off" through a similar approach, Native people in the North were quick to reject the government's simplistic "cash for land" approach. They recognized that cash alone would not protect their long-term interests. Their lands and communities were being threatened by a development process orchestrated by outsiders for the benefit of outsiders; if their cultures were to survive, they would have to secure some degree of ongoing control over the lands upon which they depended.

Their strategy for obtaining that control was to include political rights on the land claims agenda. Only by the recognition of their political rights, it was argued, could they hope to control the nature, pace and location of development on their lands. Only by acquiring political rights could they be assured that decisions would be made in the interests of northerners versus southerners, and especially in the interests of natives versus non-natives. "No pipeline before a land claims settlement" became the slogan which conveyed their determination to secure those rights before any development took place. While the Inuit pursued this strategy through their Nunavut proposal, it was the Dene Nation which expressed the demand for political rights with the greatest eloquence and force. The Dene Declaration of 1975 was a landmark event in the evolution of Native politics in the North.

The government was having none of it. Federal politicians went out of their way to ridicule the Dene Declaration, calling it "gobbledegook," and federal negotiators were prohibited from discussing political rights beyond the local level. Native groups were quick to recognize the limitations inherent in the government response. They realized that unless they gained some degree of ongoing control over their regional economies, they could never exercise control over developments with the greatest impacts on their communities and culture. Despite government attempts to bully them (by labelling their demands "separatist" and "Marxist," and cutting funding at strategic moments), the Native groups refused to back down. The result was a stalemate in negotiations which lasted throughout the rest of the 1970s.

By the early 1980s, the strategies of the Native groups began to shift. This was a result of changes – economic and political – that had been occurring in the North. The issues in the early 1970s were: What kind of development should take place in the North? and even more important: Who was going to decide? By the early 1980s these questions were mostly resolved. While Native people were still holding out at the claims table for the political rights needed to control development, the federal government was implementing the model of development it preferred from the outset. While none of the proposed energy mega-projects got off the ground, Ottawa did bankroll the oil and gas industry with billions of dollars of subsidies and write-offs throughout the 1970s, and put in place the infrastructure to support large-scale resource exploitation. The issues of whether this type of activity would be allowed, and on whose terms, were decided by default. The inability of the Native groups to stop development pending the resolution of their claims had become increasingly apparent. The only attempt by a Native group to challenge the government's development activities in court during this time – the Inuit of Baker Lake in 1979 – failed to meet its primary objective.

Once it became clear development was going to happen even in the absence of a settlement, pressure began to grow at the community level to resolve claims to "catch a ride" on the development that was occurring. This was especially the case in those areas under the greatest pressure from the development – the Mackenzie Valley and Beaufort regions. This pressure contributed to the decision by the Dene in 1980 to support the construction of the Norman Wells pipeline, even though no progress had been made on their claims. It was also the major factor behind the COPE settlement in 1984. "No pipeline before a land claims settlement" was clearly a strategy that had not worked.

One factor that allowed Native groups to gradually concede the issue of political rights at the land claims table was the emergence in 1979 of a Native majority in the Legislative Assembly of the N.W.T. This trend gave rise to the hope that the G.N.W.T. could provide an alternate vehicle by which natives might obtain, if not political rights (in the aboriginal sense), at least political control (in electoral terms). The Inuit carried this strategy furthest. In 1979, they made a decision to separate their quest for political rights from the land claims process, and to pursue political control through the creation of a Nunavut territory where Inuit would make up the majority of the voting population.

With political rights gone from the land claims table, negotiations progressed more quickly. This did not imply that Native groups were any more willing to accept the government's original cash for land offer. Led by the Inuit, they pushed for a strong role in the management of lands and resources at the regulatory level. The government had no problem with the creation of innumerable "advisory" boards (it had set up dozens in the Inuvialuit settlement in the Beaufort Sea region), but the Inuit and Dene wanted more: an equal say in regulatory bodies that would have actual decision-making powers over land use planning, water management, and the impact review process relating to development projects. If the central struggle of the 1970s was over political rights, the equivalent struggle of the 1980s was over management rights.

It was against this backdrop that the Conservatives came to power in 1984. While most observers predicted a "get tough" approach to claims from the new government, its first moves proved surprising. Perhaps the greatest surprise was the appointment of David Crombie as Minister of DIAND. Crombie had been a popular mayor of Toronto in the 1970s but, while successful as a politician, he had virtually no background in Native issues. What he brought to the job was a populist style, an enthusiastic attitude, and a relatively open mind. He also surrounded himself with a team of advisors experienced in, and sympathetic to, Native rights issues.

One of Crombie's first acts as minister was to set up a task force to review the government's comprehensive land claims policy, in the hope of overcoming the inertia that had characterized the process during the Liberal years. To conduct the review, Crombie drew once again upon experts who were knowledgeable of, and even sympathetic to, the Native cause.

The task force's report – *Living Treaties: Lasting Agreements*[80] – was sweeping in scope. It called not just for a new policy on comprehensive claims, but an entirely "new relationship" between the government and Native people in Canada. Comprehensive claims, it said, should not be approached as once-and-for-all cash for land transactions, but rather as "a first step" toward "the building of self-sufficient aboriginal communities." It argued: "The new policy should encourage aboriginal communities to become not only economically self-sufficient but also to establish political and social institutions that will allow them to become self-governing." It called for agreements which would be "living" documents and "flexible" over time, "to allow for growth and to meet the changing needs of aboriginal communities and Canadian societies." It argued strongly that Native people should "share in the financial rewards of development on their traditional territories," because "political power is meaningless without the backing of financial resources." Finally, it stated that Native people should not be made to surrender totally their aboriginal rights as a precondition for settlements.

The task force report, not surprisingly, was hailed by many Native people and their supporters as visionary. In the months following its release, an intensive lobbying effort was undertaken to build political, bureaucratic and public support for its recommendations. Unfortunately, by this time, the minister who sponsored the policy review lost much of his enthusiasm for the issue. The complex and seemingly intractable nature of Native problems was too much even for David Crombie's populist and enthusiastic approach. There could be no "quick fixes" to Native problems, and Crombie increasingly wanted out. Near the mid-way point in the Conservatives' term, before any new policy recommendations were taken to Cabinet, he got his wish.

The man who replaced Crombie as the new Minister of Indian and Northern Affairs was Bill McKnight, a straight-talking farmer from Saskatchewan with no outward interest in, or sympathy for, Native concerns. In terms of style, he was Crombie's opposite. He had no interest in mingling with or learning from the people he was supposed to be serving, and was more inclined to take direction from his department's bureaucrats. His main concerns were to tighten up the financial administration of his department, and keep Native issues out of the headlines.

McKnight had the responsibility for taking recommendations for a new land claims policy to Cabinet. The resulting new policy, announced in December 1986, reflects little of the vision of the Coolican Report. It avoids much of the discussion about the broader goals of comprehensive land claims – to develop self-sufficient, self-governing Native communities – and contents itself with a clearer delineation of what will be negotiable at the comprehensive claims table.

This greater clarity has the potential to be a positive step. The old policy was plagued by vagueness, resulting in federal negotiators running back to Cabinet for directions every time an innovative proposal was placed before them. The new policy eliminated this vagueness to a large degree, but often in a regressive way.

On the positive side, the new policy opens the door for the first time to the negotiation of matters long sought by Native groups: joint decision-making over lands and resources, resource revenue-sharing, and the offshore. The government's restrictive application of the new policy has meant that Native groups have sometimes been left worse off than before.

In terms of resource revenue-sharing, the new policy continues to reflect the view that claims settlements are really only a mechanism for "buying Native people out." Instead of recognizing that Native people have a legitimate, ongoing right to benefit from resources on or under their lands, the new policy imposes limits on how much they might benefit from resource revenues. The only new thing Ottawa is willing to negotiate is the formula by which such benefits can be capped (by fixed dollar amount, by time frame, or by a reduced royalty percentage). At the same time, Native groups are being told that any gains derived from resource revenues will ultimately be taken from other parts of the settlement package – compensation. The new policy is not designed to provide Native people with a greater financial base; it merely expands the range of options by which they can be "bought off."

Regarding the potential arrangements for jointly managing lands and resources, the story is the same. While the new policy recognizes "aboriginal interests in relation to environmental concerns particularly as those concerns relate to wildlife management and the use of water and land," it backs away from an acknowledgement of any rights. At the same time, it reaffirms the government's determination to "protect the interests of all users, to ensure resource conservation . . . and to manage renewable resources within its jurisdiction."

While Ottawa is willing to consider at least a superficial Native role in the management of lands and resources, it still prefers such a role to remain "advisory," with the government retaining the final say over development. The only new twist is that it is willing to negotiate a guaranteed role for Native people on any public bodies dealing with land and resource issues. The downside of this offer is that the eventual powers of such bodies will be decided by the government. As long as this remains the case, it is unlikely that such boards will ever be given any independent authority or regulatory teeth.

The new policy also brought clarity as to what will not be negotiated at the claims table. Native groups exploited the vagueness of the old policy by loading the agenda with every conceivable item they could think of, in the hope of making claims settlements the basis for a broad "social contract" between themselves and other Canadians. The new policy has brought an end to this hope. The Conservatives have made it explicit that comprehensive claims are primarily about land and not much else. They have rejected the negotiation of language rights, health and social provisions, or broadcasting rights under the new policy. More pointedly, they have refused to negotiate anything which might constitute a new and ongoing program at the claims table. Tragically, this includes hunter income support programs which have proven cost-efficient and culturally reinforcing in the areas where they have been established (James Bay and Northern Quebec).

The government's unwillingness to consider any new ongoing rights or jurisdictions is another indication of its continuing "buy out" attitude toward claims. Despite the Coolican Report's call for settlements which will be "living agreements" and "flexible" over time, the government continues to hold to the view that claims are a "once-and-for-all" transaction, with a fixed and preferably limited cost. The policy of avoiding any new ongoing program expenditures as a result of claims settlements is another example of the government's determination to limit its long-term financial obligations to Native people in Canada.

The new Tory policy can be said to represent "one step forward, and two steps back" for Native people attempting to negotiate comprehensive land claims settlements. The Conservatives have succeeded in eliminating much of the ambiguity of the previous Liberal policy and the result, with a few notable exceptions, has been to narrow the basis on which claims can be negotiated. This narrowing can be attributed to two factors: Ottawa's determination to retain public control over resource development at the regulatory and political levels; and its determination to avoid any long-term, open-ended financial commitments to Native people.

Looking back over the last 20 years, Ottawa has been successful at implementing much of its original agenda on the claims front. In the North, it put into place the model of development it preferred from the outset, especially as it pertains to the resource development sector. Through successive land claims policies, it prevented Native people from intruding on its exclusive control over the development process – at least on the basis of their aboriginal rights. It achieved the latter by successfully preventing Native groups from negotiating political rights at the land claims table throughout the 1970s, and by resisting attempts to negotiate a meaningful share of management responsibilities at the regulatory level in the 1980s. The Inuit of the Eastern Arctic have probably gone furthest under the existing policy, but even there the joint management regulatory bodies will remain subject to a final ministerial override.

Amazon North?:
The Continuing Loss of Native Lands

Distance brings morality into focus.

As the 1980s came to a close, the attention of Canadians was increasingly drawn to events in the Amazon rainforest of Brazil. The efforts of resource developers, enthusiastically supported by the government to open up regions of uncharted rainforest, were being monitored with growing concern. Attention was directed at the environmental degradation resulting from the clearcutting of the rainforest – from the destruction of river ecosystems following the construction of dams for hydro-electric purposes, and from pollution caused by mining and other industrial activities. Attention was also focused on the impacts of these so-called development activities on the indigenous people of the region: the introduction of new diseases, the loss of their traditional land base, the rapid decline in their ability to pursue traditional activities and to control their own destiny.

Two aspects of the public debate surrounding these issues and events have been noteworthy:

First, the focus of attention has clearly been on the patterns in the development process underway in the Amazon region. While individual projects and/or groups of individual indigenous peoples are mentioned, it is done to illustrate trends related to the overall assault on the physical environment, and its deleterious impact on the local inhabitants. Attention to these patterns has also made clear the close structural relationship between government and industry in opening up a new frontier, a process which involves a systematic assault on areas of traditional Native land use.

The other striking aspect of the attention paid to these events and issues – particularly by mainstream media – is the extent to which an explicit moral judgment has been rendered on the events in the Amazon, and about the actions of the players involved. There has been a clear willingness – unusual for the mainstream press – to both name and condemn the exploiters (resource developers, in conjunction with the government), and to identify the victims (indigenous people and the environment) in unequivocal terms.

If distance tends to bring out the essential moral issues, the people of Brazil are in a better position than Canadians to understand events taking place within our own country. While our media may be more reluctant to identify the patterns, or to render moral judgment about the players, a major assault is also underway in Canada against the remaining lands still being used in traditional ways to sustain aboriginal people. This assault, spanning the northern parts of the provinces from B.C. to Labrador, is comparable in every way with the patterns prevalent in the Brazilian rainforest: in scale; in the role played by giant resource companies; in the active support provided by federal and provincial governments; in the devastating impact of these activities on the physical environment; and in the negative, sometimes genocidal, consequences for the indigenous population.

The elements of this assault include:

1. *Forestry*: The 1980s have witnessed an unprecedented advancement by the forest industry into the northern regions of the provinces – the last areas where aboriginal people have sustained themselves from land-based activities. This corporate move northward – for logging and pulp and paper – has been precipitated by the gradual depletion of forest reserves in the southern regions, and the development of new technologies which have rendered certain tree species common in the North (notably aspen) commercially usable.

The scale of this advancement has been staggering. In B.C., forest giants such as Fletcher Challenge, Great Lakes Forest Products, and MacMillan Bloedel have been applying for cutting rights in northern areas that are up to twice the size of Vancouver Island.[81] In Alberta, in what has been called "the great boreal land rush,"[82] approximately one-third of the province's territory has been leased to pulp and paper companies since late 1987.[83] In Manitoba, a single company has obtained cutting rights to approximately one-fifth of the province.[84]

Provincial governments have been more than active supporters of this corporate advancement into the remote regions. In addition to subsidizing companies indirectly (through the provision of publicly financed infrastructure such as roads), they have directed huge amounts of public funds into the coffers of private companies to ensure adequate profit margins are maintained. In Alberta, an estimated $1 billion in grants and loan guarantees was provided to pulp and paper companies during an 18-month period in the late 1980s, even though its own Ministry of Forestry admitted that "some of the major projects might have proceeded without government involvement."[85] Governments have also started to give large corporations exclusive rights to manage vast areas of forest on a long-term (25-year) basis. This shift to a "tree farm" approach to licensing represents a massive privatization of one of the most essential public resources in Canada.

The effect of this northward expansion by the forestry industry has been to repeat both the earlier experience in the South, and the current experience in the Amazon. The environmental degradation caused by clearcutting – soil erosion and the depletion of wildlife – often combines with the extensive use of herbicides and pesticides to alter the ecosystem on which life has depended. The construction of new roads into previously inaccessible regions not only affects the movement of big game animals, but also introduces outsiders eager to compete with the indigenous population for a share of an increasingly scarce resource.

2. *Hydro-Electric Development*: Similar to Brazil, the hydro- electric potential of Canada's fresh water river systems is immense. In Canada, as in Brazil, this potential is rapidly being tapped by a system of dams and diversions which is destroying the traditional land base of centuries-old Native cultures.

The first string of dams designed to tap the flow of major northern rivers and waterways was largely in place by the 1970s: Churchill Falls in Labrador, James Bay in Quebec, the Churchill and Reindeer Rivers in northern Manitoba and Saskatchewan, and the Peace River in B.C. The effect of these projects has been disastrous for many Native groups and communities. The flooding of traditional lands has meant the destruction of vital wildlife habitats, as well as the immediate displacement of the people from areas of long-standing economic and spiritual significance. The manipulation of water levels to suit the fluctuating energy demands of southern consumers has often prevented the re-establishment of communities at different locations along the same river systems.

The destruction of their traditional economic base – which always afforded them a high degree of self-sufficiency and independence – inevitably had an impact on the social and psychological life of Native communities. Wherever displacement has occurred, increased dependency on welfare has tended to follow, along with increases in alcohol abuse, family breakdown and suicide. If compensation was offered for the loss of resources and traditional lifestyles, it was usually as an afterthought, sometimes long after the dams had been built, and occasionally only after governments were forced by the courts.

If many of the above consequences were predictable, one major impact was not: the natural release of mercury into the water, and eventually into the food chain, through the decomposition of organic matter in the flooded areas. The result has been a dramatic rise in the level of mercury in Native people in areas such as James Bay, with unknown, long-term consequences for their physical health. Although evidence of this phenomenon is now incontrovertible, provincial governments such as that of Quebec continue to look for ways to expand their hydro-electric capacity, often only to export it to the United States. Also, financial compensation does not take into consideration the loss of culture or lifestyle.

Despite the undeniably negative consequences for Native peoples, provincial governments across the country are now embarking on another round of hydro-electric developments. In Quebec, this includes plans to dam the Ashuapmuchuan River near Lac St. Jean to provide electricity for aluminum smelters, as well as the completion of James Bay II on the Great Whale and the Nottaway-Broadback-Rupert river systems – intended to provide power for export to the United States. Manitoba Hydro is planning the construction of the Canawapa generating station on the lower Nelson River for the purposes of selling electricity to Ontario. Next door in Saskatchewan, the provincial power corporation is planning to build a replacement for a 60-year old dam on the Churchill River which has wreaked havoc on two Native communities downstream because of continually fluctuating water levels.

3. *Oil and Gas Development*: One cannot fly over the northern part of Alberta without being struck by the almost never-ending grid of cut lines which dissects the remote boreal forest. These cut lines are the mark of an oil and gas industry which has invaded northern Alberta in the last decade. Nowhere has the dramatic and devastating impact of this invasion been more evident than in the case of the Lubicon Cree.

Until the 1970s, the Lubicon Cree were isolated from, and unaffected by, the activities of the industrial society of the South. The network of families that made up the band continued to live largely traditional lifestyles, with moose and deer the primary game animals around which their hunting revolved.

The construction of an all-weather road into their region during the 1970s brought an end not only to their isolation, but their health and self-reliance as a people. Between 1979 and 1982, more than 400 oil and gas wells were drilled within a 15-mile radius of their community. This sudden, massive intrusion onto their land had a quick and devastating impact on the wildlife population on which the Lubicon had been dependent. The number of moose killed for food dropped from an average of 200 per year to less than 20; annual income from trapping dropped from an average of $5,000 per trapper to less than $400.[86] Not surprisingly, this rapid decline in their traditional economic base also had devastating human consequences. Dependence on welfare rose from 10 per cent in 1981 to more than 95 per cent in 1983; alcohol abuse and suicide rates have soared; and "third world" diseases such as tuberculosis have re-emerged in almost epidemic proportions. While the people were suffering these effects, the oil companies were removing an estimated $1 million a day from their land.[87]

4. *Militarization*: Resource developers have not been the only ones guilty of eroding the traditional land base of aboriginal people in Canada. Governments, on occasion, have been the principal instigators of activities that have undermined the continued use of traditional lands. One contemporary example is the increased use of remote areas for military purposes.

The most glaring use of Native lands for military purposes has been in Nitassinan, or Labrador, where CFB Goose Bay was recently developed into a base for several European countries wanting to train fighter pilots in low-level flying techniques. This technique is to equip NATO allies with the capability of reaching enemy territory without being detected by radar. While justified as a "defensive strategy" – it would supposedly allow NATO to counter-attack if its missiles were demobilized – critics argue that its real intent is to strengthen the "first strike" capability of the Western Alliance. The use of cruise missiles in the recent Gulf War only confirmed this fear.

The use of CFB Goose Bay as a low-level training base began in 1980 and has expanded steadily over the past decade, with the number of flights increasing from 3,000 in 1984 to 7,000 in 1987 over lands traditionally used by the Innu.[88] This activity has had a serious impact on the caribou of the region, particularly the George River herd, which scientists estimate to be declining at a rate of five per cent per year since 1984.[89] The psychological trauma on the Innu has been no less severe. As the pastor in one community described it: "There is a collective psychosis which is undermining the heart and way of life of the Indians."[90]

Despite a decade of protests against this activity, the federal government had aggressively promoted the region as the site for a future NATO

Tactical Fighter and Weapons Training Centre. Such a development would have increased the low-level flights each year to approximately 40,000 over 100,000 square kilometres of Innu land. It would also have involved the establishment of nine practice bombing ranges, at least two of which would have been used with live ammunition. It is felt by many that advent of this development would have led to the complete destruction of traditional Innu society and culture. Despite its efforts to downplay the impact of the Innu protestors, Canada's bid was eventually defeated and the facility was awarded to Turkey. The use of the region for low-flight training, however, persists, and will be maintained at present levels.

While the scale of military activity is greatest in Nitassinan, it is not the only area in Canada where traditional Native lands are being affected by military activities. A bombing range at Primrose Lake in northern Alberta and Saskatchewan has removed approximately three million acres of land from traditional use and occupancy. In addition to the use of the Mackenzie Valley corridor for cruise missile testing, other flight corridors have been established in parts of British Columbia, northern Ontario, Alberta, Saskatchewan, the North West Territories and New Brunswick for use by the North American Air Defense's (NORAD) Strategic Air Command. Plans call for up to twenty-five B-52 and B1-B bombers to fly through these corridors at levels as low as 100 metres, four times a year, with squadrons of up to fifteen F-111 jet fighters practising interceptions.[91] Similar activities have also been on the increase over Inuit regions in the far North. Since 1986, NORAD has been conducting exercises twice a year in Iqaluit, using CF-18s and other military aircraft. By 1993, it is estimated that such exercises will be conducted out of at least five other northern communities.[92]

Going to Court:
Certain Costs, Uncertain Benefits

Over the last 20 years, the courts have been used increasingly by aboriginal people as a strategic tool, either to force the government to come to the negotiating table, or as a last line of defence when all attempts to negotiate have failed. Despite some historic victories, the courts have not been a reliable alternative to negotiations in resolving grievances. A variety of factors have contributed to this uncertain result:

First, going to court has always run the risk of being prohibitively expensive. Lawyers with specialized expertise in Native law seldom come cheaply (legal fees for lawyers representing the government in land claims litigation in B.C. have run as high as $6,000 per day); court costs can be astronomical (an estimated $800 per hour); and the depth of legal and historical research required to build a successful case is often far greater than in "normal" litigation practice.[93] Marginalized groups out to establish and/or defend their legal interests are not typically endowed with the financial resources needed to engage in lengthy court actions, and cannot compete with governments that have almost unlimited access to the public purse. For reasons of cost alone, the courts have never been an option entered into lightly.

Money spent by Ottawa to ensure its legal obligations to Native people are kept to a minimum is almost impossible to calculate because some expenditures are more traceable than others. The amount paid to private law firms hired to represent the government in litigation provides one indication of the lengths to which the government is prepared to go. Recent records show the federal government has been spending more money to fight Native land claims than any other issue. In 1988-89, the law firm that billed the Department of Justice the most money in Canada was Koenigsberg and Russell of Vancouver, whose primary job was to fight three high profile claims in B.C. The third highest bill was from MacAuley and McColl, also of Vancouver, which shared the workload on the same three claims. The fourth highest billing came from Black & Co. of Calgary, which represented the government in its negotiations with the Lubicon. In short, three of the top four highest billing private law firms in Canada were engaged in fighting aboriginal people in court.[94] Aboriginal groups, by comparison, have often had to rely on "feasts, public appeals, raffles, bingos, etc." to raise funds to fully present their case during even the first round of court action.[95]

The amounts paid to private law firms are nowhere near the figure Ottawa spends to defend itself against Native people. The Department of Justice maintains its own internal Native Law Section to track and assess events and decisions relating to a myriad of issues associated with Native law: land rights; treaty rights (pre-Confederation and post-Confederation); hunting rights; resource rights (to fish, timber, wildlife, oil and gas, wild rice); constitutional rights; and taxation. This section provides the government with strategic advice on how to deal with legal actions emanating from the Native community. The Department of Justice also maintains a Legal Services Branch within each federal department, including those directly affected by Native claims (Indian Affairs, Environment and Fisheries). In Indian Affairs, in particular, so much legal defence work is done that a special Legal Liaison and Support Branch has been created to co-ordinate the government's response.

Another factor that has weighed against the courts as a reliable option for Native groups is the time it can take to obtain a definitive ruling.

The experience of the Teme-Augama Anishnabai, or Bear Island Band, is one example. The band took the first step to assert legal jurisdiction over its traditional homelands in northeastern Ontario in 1973. After failed attempts to resolve the dispute through negotiation, the case went to trial in the Supreme Court of Ontario in 1982. Two years later, after 119 days of proceedings, the court ruled against the band's claim. The band appealed, but it took five more years before the Appeal Court of Ontario issued its ruling, which again went against the band. The band has since decided to attempt an appeal to the Supreme Court of Canada, which means it could take a decade to get a final court decision.

The experience of the Gitksan-Wet'suwet'en Tribal Council in B.C. will likely exceed that of the Teme-Augama Anishnabai, at least in the time it could take to resolve its case in the courts. Frustrated by the ongoing exploitation of their lands in northwestern B.C., and by the refusal of the B.C. government to enter any form of negotiation, the Gitksan-Wet'suwet'en have undertaken what will inevitably be a long, legal process to assert legal rights over their land. In suing the B.C. government for full title to their traditional homelands they are hoping to affirm not only that their aboriginal title still exists, but that it gives them complete political jurisdiction over those lands. Achieving this goal could take even longer than in the case of the Teme-Augama Anishnabai.

The Gitksan-Wet'suwet'en began their court action in 1984. Because of the complexity of the case and the significance of the legal issues involved, it took almost three years to prepare the evidence for the trial (up to 10,000 documents were eventually examined by the court), and another three years (more than 300 sitting days) to present it. The initial ruling by the B.C. Supreme Court was handed down in March, 1991. The ruling, couched in surprisingly colonial terms, categorically rejected the notion of aboriginal title. An appeal is likely. If the dispute proceeds to the Supreme Court of Canada, it could take more than a decade to reach a resolution.

In addition to being both time consuming and expensive, using the courts to achieve a resolution to outstanding claims can also be highly risky. Unlike a negotiation process, in which both sides are assured of an outcome that will meet some of their needs, the court process has the potential to create clear winners and losers. To "go for broke" in the courts can mean winning big, but it can also mean losing big, and losing once-and-for-all. While the prospect of winning big is tantalizing to both sides, the prospect of losing big keeps most players from pushing the court process to its limits.

In this high-stakes game of legal poker, there is probably no better or more important example than the issue of aboriginal "title." While the notion of an aboriginal "interest" in the land has been an integral part of British law since the Royal Proclamation of 1763, the precise legal meaning of this interest or title has never been fully delineated by the courts. In the absence of any definitive ruling, the question of who actually owns much of the land in Canada remains theoretically up for grabs. This uncertainty applies particularly to those areas of the country where aboriginal title has never been explicitly extinguished by any treaty: most of B.C., the Yukon and the North West Territories, Northern Quebec (before 1975), and Labrador.

The government's first line of defence against the assertion of aboriginal rights was to argue that the concept was too archaic to be treated seriously in a modern liberal, democratic society. This particular position was expressed with great clarity and even bluntness by Prime Minister Trudeau as recently as 1969,[96] but was shot down by the Supreme Court of Canada in its 1973 Calder decision, which confirmed that aboriginal title was still a viable concept even in twentieth century society.

The second line of defence used by governments to deny the present day existence of an aboriginal title was to argue that it only existed in those areas which had been explicitly covered by the Royal Proclamation: the areas immediately surrounding the Great Lakes and Nova Scotia. Two legal questions were at stake. First, would the principles outlined in the Proclamation have applied to other parts of what is now Canada if these areas had been known at the time? Second, does the present day recognition of aboriginal title even depend on the Royal Proclamation? Once again, the court action initiated by the Nisga'a moved the issue forward. For a combination of reasons, the Supreme Court of Canada affirmed in 1973 that it was possible for an aboriginal title to exist in those areas of Canada beyond the original geographic scope of the Proclamation – at least theoretically.

This situation left open the question of whether such a title actually does exist today in those areas. The only way it could not exist is if it had been extinguished in some legally acceptable manner. British law traditionally recognized three ways by which this could be done: by conquest, by treaty, or being superseded by other laws. Because aboriginal people in Canada were never conquered, the first was not a factor. In those areas of the country where treaties had clearly not been signed, the question boiled down to whether aboriginal rights had ever been superseded by government laws. In other words, could an aboriginal right still be said to exist in areas where the government had long been exercising what seemed to be complete jurisdiction?

One technical question which had to be answered was whether extinguishment had to be done explicitly to be legitimate. In the case of the

Nisga'a, the B.C. government argued that any aboriginal title that might have existed would have been automatically extinguished when B.C. entered Confederation – when jurisdiction over the land was handed to the province. The Nisga'a argued that in the absence of any explicit statement of intent, extinguishment could not be presumed to have happened. On this critical question, the Nisga'a fell short of achieving a legal victory; the top court split on the issue of whether extinguishment had to be done explicitly or directly, or whether it could be accomplished as a consequence of the government's other legislative activity.

Beyond the question of whether an aboriginal right exists is the matter of what it could mean. What are the rights that would flow from an aboriginal interest in the land? Would they provide aboriginal people only with the right to pursue so-called traditional activities: hunting, fishing and trapping? If so, would these activities still be subject to government regulation? Would an aboriginal title include the right to own the land "lock, stock, and barrel" to the point of being able to exclude others from it? Or would an aboriginal title merely imply the right to use land that would otherwise belong to the Crown? The courts have barely started to answer these substantive questions, in part because both sides have been reluctant to ask for a definitive ruling. The stakes are so high, neither side wants to risk the possibility of losing.

Against this backdrop, the significance of the current Gitksan Wet'suwet'en court battle can be understood. Frustrated by the B.C. government's refusal to acknowledge their rights, they have made the decision to "go for broke" in the courts. They have asked the court to affirm not only that their aboriginal title still exists, but that it confers on them the political powers needed to exercise jurisdiction over their homelands. In effect, they are seeking to resolve in one action the most central legal issue in the aboriginal rights arena. Whatever the result, the decision will likely have enormous implications for aboriginal law throughout Canada.

Even if the Gitksan-Wet'suwet'en were to win big in court, it would not guarantee their victory on the ground. The sad truth, when it comes to Native people, is that Canadian governments have a long record of not obeying their own laws. In the case of the treaties, there have been an almost endless list of cases in which the government has failed to adhere to its legal obligations. Either it has not provided the lands required under its own treaties, or it has failed to manage Indian lands and assets according to the standards required under the Constitution.

This pattern of resistance continues, and can be seen in the way governments have responded to the significant legal victories achieved by aboriginal people. Faced with unfavourable rulings, governments have responded by ignoring or minimizing their policy implications.

In one case that went to the Supreme Court of Canada in 1984, an Indian band from B.C. won a ruling that was thought to change forever the assumptions about the government's trust responsibilities toward Indians. Under the BNA Act of 1867, and through subsequent versions of the Indian Act, the federal government had assumed a trust responsibility for "Indians and lands reserved for Indians." For more than a century, Ottawa operated on the assumption that this trust responsibility was only political, and could not be enforced in the courts. When the Supreme Court of Canada ruled on the claim by the Musqueam band that their lands had been sold for less than full value, the legal ground shifted dramatically. The court ruled in decisive terms that the government's obligations to look after the best interests of Indians were legally enforceable, and should meet the highest standards of accountability. Despite the clear, sweeping tone of the ruling, the Department of Justice has made every attempt to minimize its impact, arguing that it only has implications for cases which conform precisely with the circumstances which gave rise to the Musqueam band's action.

Throughout the 1980s, the top courts have repeatedly asserted that Indian treaties should be interpreted liberally, and in cases of doubt, in favour of the Indians. The courts have shown increasing willingness to apply this approach themselves, with the result that the rules of evidence have become less strict; the onus on the government to prove extinguishment has increased; and the definition of what constitutes a legally valid treaty has been broadened. Once again, these positive developments on the legal front have not always been translated into changes in government policy.

Perhaps the most glaring example of the potential futility of using the courts is the case of the Micmac Indians of Nova Scotia. The forefathers of the current Micmacs signed treaties with colonial powers as early as the 1700s. These treaties were little more than "peace and friendship" agreements, to ensure that each side could pursue its respective economic activities without fear of interference from the other. The primary economic activity of the Micmacs was hunting and fishing.

With the expansion of the colonial society and the advent of Confederation, the ability of Micmac Indians to pursue their traditional activities was gradually restricted. Once it was in a dominant position, the white society quickly lost interest in respecting the content of past treaties, and felt free to pass laws and regulations which ran counter to their intent. By the mid-20th century, the assumption in the dominant society was that such treaties were irrelevant and invalid. This view was given official expression in the federal government's 1973 policy statement on comprehensive claims. While the new policy expressed a willingness to consider the claims of aboriginal people who had never signed treaties, and to "honour lawful obligations" arising from agreements, it precluded consideration of claims arising from pre-Confederation treaties in the Maritimes and southern Quebec.

Fed up with the aggressive enforcement of provincial fish and game laws, the Micmacs finally opted to go to court to reassert the validity of their treaties. At first, it appeared that this strategy of "going for broke" in the courts had paid off. In 1985, the Supreme Court of Canada issued a landmark ruling stating that the Micmacs' treaty rights to hunt and fish were still valid. Despite this ruling from the country's highest court, the actions of the provincial government have barely changed – Indians continue to be harassed, arrested and jailed for their hunting practices. After going through the court system to establish the law, the Micmacs are now repeating the process to get the government to obey it. After the Nova Scotia Supreme Court Appeals Division threw out subsequent charges for illegal salmon fishing in 1990, the provincial government finally threw in the towel and agreed to stop its prosecutions; but not before the Native organizations were left "financially crippled." [97]

The federal government's willingness to obey the courts' direction will continue to be tested in the years ahead. In May 1990, the Supreme Court of Canada issued its first historic interpretation of the meaning of Section 35 (1) of the new Constitution. (This section is the clause in which "the existing aboriginal and treaty rights of the aboriginal peoples of Canada are hereby recognized and affirmed"). The issue was whether a member of the Musqueam Indian Band in Britich Columbia, Ronald Sparrow, had an aboriginal right to fish which overrode regulations imposed by the *Fisheries Act*. The Court ruled in Sparrow's favour, and in addition, made clear that "the government is required to bear the burden of justifying *any* legislation that has some negative effect on *any* aboriginal right protected under S. 35 (1)" *[emphasis mine]*. In other words, the onus is now on the government to consider aboriginal rights in the development of all its laws and regulations, and to provide strong reasons why any of its laws should be allowed to diminish aboriginal rights. Despite the clear and sweeping tone of this ruling, however, the federal government probably will continue to pass its laws and leave it up to aboriginal groups to challenge their validity in the courts.

"As Long As The Sun Shines . . .":
The Current Conjuncture for Native People

The sun is setting on an entire era of Native politics in Canada.

To understand the significance of this point, it is best to look upon the events of the last two decades in a generational context. In many respects, the emergence of the current group of Native leaders was the result of the government's own bungling. The 1969 White Paper exhibited such a gross degree of duplicity that a generation of young Native people was awakened to the need to defend itself from the assimilationist tendencies of a white man's government.

The intent of this new generation of young leaders was to test whether their "system" could work to the advantage of aboriginal people. Organizations that were formed quickly in response to the White Paper had become, by the end of the decade, established institutions capable of representing Native interests on a variety of policy and program issues; lobbying skills were refined to a point where these organizations became accepted players on the national political scene; youthful leaders became skilled and articulate advocates for the Native cause, equal in ability to the best of non-Native politicians.

For a while, the results of their efforts were sufficient to provide Native people with a basis for optimism about their ability to achieve success through established channels. During the 1970s and early 1980s, significant new avenues for dealing with the government were opened to deal with long-standing problems. In 1973, a process was established for settling both comprehensive and specific claims; for several years in the 1970s, a joint First Nations/Cabinet committee was operating to give Native leaders direct access to senior federal politicians; in the early 1980s, a recognition of aboriginal rights was secured in the Constitution, leading to an unprecedented series of constitutional talks with the First Ministers of Canada.

These new forums were directly attributable to the work of the generation of leaders who had emerged in response to the White Paper. During this period, the courts had also been employed with strategic effectiveness, further demonstrating the ability of aboriginal people to use the system to their own advantage. The evidence during the 1970s and early 1980s suggested that with enough determination, persistence and professionalism in political lobbying and legal manoeuvring, their aspirations might eventually be met by working within the system.

By the end of the Conservatives' first term of office, this mood of optimism had all but evaporated. The failure of the constitutional talks, the new restrictions imposed by the long-awaited land claims policy, the extremely restrictive scope of the government's self-government policy, the cynical indifference toward specific claims, the determination to avoid new costs and reduce existing ones, the willingness of the justice department and provincial governments to ignore the implications of hard-won court battles – all of these factors were providing stiff lessons about what the system was willing or able to deliver.

As the 1980s came to a close, it was becoming increasingly apparent that things were no longer moving forward. While aboriginal communities were exhorted to become more "self-sufficient," governments in Canada were acting to systematically reduce their access to resources – either through direct cuts in spending, or through the assault on their traditional land base. The effect of this policy trend will be, in fact, remarkably similar to the South African government's drive to create supposedly "independent" black homelands, where blacks are "given" an inadequate land base on which to live (in size and material resources), are denied access to suitable financial resources, then told they are "free" to govern themselves completely – meaning the government accepts no more political, economic, or legal responsibility for them.

While these trends were becoming clear, a new generation of potential leaders was beginning to emerge that could see the limited results of playing by the rules. The Conservative government's announced funding cuts for post-secondary education in the spring of 1989 may galvanize this new generation into activism, much as the White Paper did for the generation 20 years ago. Whatever it takes for them to coalesce, the strategy of this new generation will be influenced by the successes – and failures – of the past 20 years. When Assembly of First Nations Chief Georges Erasmus recently warned: "We may be the last generation of leaders that are prepared to sit down and peacefully negotiate,"[98] it was intended more as a warning than a threat.

With the limited results of playing by the rules becoming apparent, Native groups have increasingly begun to use alternate means to achieve their goals. Asserting their jurisdiction "on the ground" has become the strategy for many groups, frustrated with the results of political negotiations, and the costs and consequences of lengthy legal battles. This trend toward direct action will lead to increased confrontations with the government, and perhaps to the alienation of public support for Native people. Given the closing down of opportunities available through more "legitimate" channels over the last eight years, should Canadians be surprised by the choices aboriginal people might make?

Of Guns and Feathers:
The Indian Summer of 1990

It took only two years for Georges Erasmus' fateful prediction to come true.

In the summer of 1990, Native communities across Canada ignited in protest to an extent, and with a degree of unity, that had never before been seen in Canada. Many of the protests were in response to the government's handling of the tense, and oftentimes violent, confrontations that were occurring between Mohawks and the police and military at Oka and Chateauguay in Quebec. Other protests were a response to the government's perpetual mishandling of innumerable other local and regional issues that had been festering for years across Canada. The many instances of "direct action" that erupted during the long, hot "Indian Summer" were a clear indication that aboriginal people were no longer willing to wait for the government to get around to dealing with their concerns. Erasmus' prediction had proven correct: the patience of aboriginal peoples was indeed running out.

The first sign of this new determination and assertiveness came in a relatively peaceful form in June, when Elijah Harper, a Cree Member of the Manitoba Legislature, clutched a sacred eagle feather and registered a simple "No" to the Manitoba government's daily request for extended hearings into the Meech Lake Accord. By withholding his support as the deadline approached, Harper effectively slammed the door on the Mulroney government's last hope for saving the beleaguered constitutional proposal.

In the process of saying "no", Harper quickly became a hero to the many different interest groups within Canada that were opposed to the controversial Accord. Even more, he became a hero to aboriginal peoples everywhere, and emerged as a symbol of their newfound determination not to be relegated to a secondary status on the country's political agenda.

The Mulroney government's message to aboriginal peoples during the entire three years of debate on the Meech Lake Accord was that their interests would be dealt with after Quebec had been persuaded to sign the constitution. But the Prime Minister's promises for the future were undermined by his own performance in the past. After all, he had already chaired two First Ministers' Conferences which had dealt exclusively with aboriginal issues (in 1985 and 1987) and neither had produced any significant results. In fact, his performance during the Meech Lake process now made it clear how uncommitted he was to achieving any deal with the provinces on aboriginal rights.

Mulroney's method of securing support for Meech Lake was to convene a meeting of the Premiers at the last possible moment and then keep them in the same room for as long as it took to get an agreement. This heavy-handed, manipulative approach to consensus-building enraged many Canadians and increased popular opposition to the Accord.

It did show, however, just how far the Prime Minister was prepared to go to get an agreement when he wanted one. It stood in dramatic contrast to his performance at the last First Ministers' Conference on aboriginal rights in 1987. That conference, after all, also had been a "last chance" opportunity – it was the last in a series of conferences that had been agreed to by the provinces back in 1983, and there was no expectation that the provinces were going to come back again after it was over. It was seen by many as perhaps the last chance in a generation to get a deal on aboriginal rights.

This time, the Prime Minister's efforts fell somewhat short of his Meech Lake style. The 1987 First Ministers' Conference had been scheduled to last two days. The first day was taken up with opening statements by the seventeen participants. As expected, the real negotiations took place on the first night of the conference. The next morning, the Prime Minister took a poll around the table, and when there was no sign of any agreement, he banged his gavel, threw up his hands in defeat, and sent everyone home early! This was not a government, or a Prime Minister, that was prepared to go to the wall for aboriginal peoples at the constitutional level.

Even if the Prime Minister's promises of future attention had credibility, however, Elijah Harper's "No" in the Manitoba legislature was a clear signal that aboriginal people were no longer willing to let their concerns be put off until some future date. It was a sign that putting aboriginal issues on the backburner was no longer going to be accepted. And his "No" to the Prime Minister's last-minute attempts to buy support with offers of Royal Commissions and the like was an equally clear signal that Native expectations were not going to be compromised.

If Elijah Harper's actions in the Manitoba legislature inspired an unprecedented degree of unity and pride among Native peoples in Canada, Oka provided the spark which turned that pride into angry action.

The original dispute – involving traditional Mohawk lands that were to be turned over to local developers for a golf course – had smouldered for months without resolution. A sudden attempt by the Quebec Provincial Police to attack the barricades in July proved a fiasco and led to the death of one police officer. Eventually the Canadian Armed Forces were called in to confront the Mohawks and to dismantle the barricades, a process which took 77 days to complete.

Despite the fact the issues underlying the Mohawk dispute – self-government, sovereignty, jurisdiction over land – had been simmering for years and even generations, the government's approach to the Oka crisis was to treat the issue as a strict "law and order" matter. By taking this approach, the government was hoping to achieve a number of public relations objectives. First, treating the individuals engaged in acts of civil disobedience as "criminals" was a way of discrediting them in the public's eye. Second, focusing on the "law and order" aspect deflected public attention away from the underlying political and economic issues which had caused the dispute in the first place. Third, it allowed the government to stake out the high moral ground – by presenting itself as the ultimate defender of law and order in our society, something all Canadians would have a stake in maintaining.

But does the government's presentation of itself as the defender of the rule of law actually stand up to examination? A close look at Canadian history might leave one asking the question: "Who are the real lawbreakers?"

For instance: In 1763, the British monarch issued a Royal Proclamation which laid down principles to govern the acquisition of Native lands by colonizers. The Proclamation declared that: 1) aboriginal peoples had certain legal rights to the lands which they traditionally used and occupied; 2) European settlers could take over Native lands and use them for other purposes only after these legal rights had been surrendered in a formal agreement such as a treaty; and 3) only the Government had the authority to negotiate such agreements.

These legal principles were the motivating factors behind the treaties that were signed in Upper Canada prior to Confederation, and across the prairies after Confederation. Following the last treaty in 1921, however, the process of treaty-making fell into a rather convenient disuse, despite the fact that European settlement and development activities continued to expand into other parts of the country. By 1969, this half-century of disuse provided the Liberal government of Pierre Trudeau with a justification for saying that the Royal Proclamation principles were no longer valid, and hence need not be applied. As we have seen, it took the actions of the Nisha'a in the Supreme Court of Canada to force the government to change its view, and to bring its actions back in line with the obligations spelled out for it by the Proclamation.

Even after it was forced by the courts to restart the treaty-making process, Ottawa has still done little to uphold the spirit and the intent of the Proclamation, especially in terms of the Crown's obligation to negotiate a deal before aboriginal lands are used by outsiders. In fact, the federal government has been one of the principal promoters of development in areas such as the North West Territories and the Yukon where valid treaties have yet to be signed, and it has used these development activities to pressure aboriginal groups into signing the kind of agreements it wants. Despite repeated requests by aboriginal groups for a halt to all development activities until after land claims agreements are reached, the government has consistently refused.

68   AND THE LAST SHALL BE FIRST

So much for upholding the rule of law, as laid down by the Royal Proclamation.

Also: Canada signed a series of land cessation treaties with First Nations across the prairies near the end of the last century. Inasmuch as these treaties solidified the government's authority over property rights in those regions, they remain a fundamental component of Canadian law. Over one hundred years after the signing of these treaties, the Canadian government still has not fulfilled all of its own legal obligations with regard to the provision of land for Reserves. The government does not dispute that it has a legal obligation to provide these lands. It just admits to being a little slow in getting around to it.

So much for upholding the law, as laid down in the treaties it has signed.

Also: In 1870, the Canadian parliament enacted the "Manitoba Act" to bring Manitoba into Confederation. Among other things, the Act provided guarantees that the Metis of the new province would receive freehold title to approximately one million four hundred thousand acres of land. The British parliament passed a law one year later ratifying the "Manitoba Act", and stipulating that the Canadian parliament would not have the authority to make any changes to it. Despite this provision, the Canadian government eventually passed various pieces of legislation which changed the rules under which land was to be allocated to Métis. As a result of these new laws, which many see as unconstitutional, Métis ended up being deprived of 85% of the land they had been promised.

So much for upholding the law, as spelled out in the government's own legislation.

In light of these various examples, it is revealing to compare the radically different responses that Native peoples and government have taken when faced with "lawbreaking". Aboriginal peoples in many parts of Canada have lived for upwards of a century with the government's refusal to adhere to its own laws. They have responded by arguing their case in any way available, using persuasion, public appeals, political pressure, legal actions, peaceful demonstrations, and when all else fails, civil disobedience. Instances of failure to uphold the law are extremely rare in aboriginal Canadian history.

When it was aboriginal people who "broke the law", however, it took the government only five weeks to send in the troops. In Canada, having an army means you can pick and choose what laws to enforce, and when.

Part 3:

The Future of Non-Native Response

The Future of Non-Native Response

From Support to Solidarity

Because the foregoing represents the current "conjuncture" with regard to Native politics in Canada, we must ask ourselves what implications does it have for the work of an inter-church coalition committed to acting in solidarity with Native people? It would be valuable to reflect upon the work of Project North, the original inter-church coalition established to deal with aboriginal issues, and be reminded of how it tried to build support among non-Native Canadians for Native rights. It will be especially important to look at the constituency Project North has always tried to mobilize, and the position of that constituency within the current conjuncture.

Project North was formed in 1975 as an inter-church coalition to provide support to aboriginal people in northern Canada whose lands were under siege from the prospect of sudden and uncontrolled mega-project developments. Project North's primary constituency has always been the middle class, inside and outside the churches. The middle class, understood in the broadest sense, was – and remains – a legitimate focus for attempts to educate and mobilize Canadians around Native rights issues because of the characteristics ascribed to it earlier. It is the group most active in electoral politics, with the knowledge, skills and resources to make itself heard, and is accustomed to a political system responsive to its needs. In short, the middle class has always played a strategic role in the workings of the electoral process in Canada, and for that reason has remained a legitimate focus for Project North's mobilizing efforts.

Following its inception in 1975, Project North was successful in cultivating and sustaining a network of Native rights support groups in urban centres across the country. These groups consisted of people who, for a variety of personal reasons, have an interest in, and hence a concern for, Native people and their position in Canadian society. While these "activists" have played an effective role in mobilizing sectors of the general public – the middle class – around particular Native struggles, their numbers have remained small. The constant challenge facing Project North was to broaden this base of interest and support beyond the level of these already committed activists. Despite its efforts, Project North was generally unsuccessful at achieving this goal during its 13-year history.

To understand the reasons for this lack of success, it is important to analyse the basis on which non-Natives have become involved in Native issues. When such involvement occurred, it was because a significant number of Canadians were alerted to a major injustice being perpetrated on Native people, and persuaded that only their active intervention could forestall it. While the support proved beneficial, even indispensable, in the context of immediate crises (dropping the aboriginal rights clause in the Constitution in 1981) and short-term struggles (the Mackenzie Valley Pipeline Inquiry), it has not provided ordinary Canadians with a basis for remaining involved. Once a particular "crisis" has been met, most Canadians return to their lives, with little or no ongoing connection to Native people and their concerns. The involvement of most Canadians in Native issues has been based primarily on altruism.

One major reason non-Native Canadians have never developed a sustained interest in Native issues is because Native problems have always been perceived as separate. People can be persuaded to give attention to Native problems if convinced that a major injustice is occurring, but the motivation for doing so arises either from a concern about their own societal self-image, or a moral concern for the plight of "others". In either case, the assumption continues that Native problems have little in common with their own. As long as this separation exists in the minds of Canadians, they can never be expected to develop an ongoing interest in, or involvement with, Native issues. By extension, they will never develop a basis for solidarity with Native people.

The conjunctural analysis presented in this book provides a basis for overcoming this separation. The primary constituency of Project North – the middle class – is under immense pressure. Economically, as the constituency shrinks, it carries an increasing share of the tax burden. Politically, it is being manipulated into a position where it will eventually give the government the "permission" it needs to dismantle the welfare state in Canada. A political wedge is being driven between the middle class and those in Canada who are dependent upon government social spending – Native people included.

Outwardly, these would not appear to be ideal conditions for organizing the middle class around Native issues, if the appeal is to be made on the basis of altruistic values. Middle class Canadians are in an increasingly insecure position within Canadian society. In the 1970s, it was easier to imagine that any gains made by Native people would be paid by someone else – corporations and government. By the end of the 1980s, the government made it clear that corporations would not be expected to pay more; in fact, they would be allowed to pay less.

It was also made increasingly clear that the costs of serving Native people or other marginal groups would be paid by the middle class. As this type of economic pressure builds on members of the middle class, they will find it increasingly difficult to "afford" an interest in the struggles of "other people", either because their energies are absorbed in keeping themselves afloat, or because they will see it as no longer in their economic interest. The environment for mobilizing Project North's main constituency, on the basis of altruism, has become increasingly hostile.

Ironically, the conditions which make it more difficult to organize the middle class in support of Native people may also provide a basis for the development of middle class solidarity with Native people. Both sectors of society are being victimized by a process intended to benefit others (wealthy individuals and large corporations). This process revolves around the government's attempt to reduce its long-term social spending, but will ultimately have more to do with the business community's desire to reduce the role of government.

In the context of the attempt to reduce social expenditures, Native people and the middle class would appear to have opposing interests. Native people are on the receiving end, while the middle class is made to pay increasing amounts. But the dynamics of the situation are more complex. The pressure being placed on the middle class will lead to increasing divisions within its ranks: between those able to survive in a free market economy and those who can't; between those able to maintain their jobs and those who won't; between the "downwardly mobile" and those able to maintain and even improve their position; between those who will become more dependent upon social programs, and those who will become less dependent.

It is likely that only the higher levels of the current middle class will survive and prosper in the context of the "new reality": professionals, managers and small business entrepreneurs. The rest of the middle class, whose income is derived from wages and who have little control over their workplace, will probably be among the victims of the restructuring that will occur in the coming decades (particularly as a result of the Free Trade Agreement and the introduction of new technologies).

The ability of the government to proceed with the corporate agenda will be determined by the political response of those in the middle class being victimized by this economic restructuring. Even as its economic position deteriorates, this group will retain much of the political efficacy characteristic of the middle class – the expectation that the political system will be responsive to its needs. How it exercises its clout will be decisive in the government's ability to realize its objectives.

One of two things could happen. If this group uses its political clout to engage in competition with other more marginalized groups for increasingly limited social program resources, the government will ultimately have its way. Whatever its circumstances, the middle class will always have the political and economic resources to compete successfully against more marginalized groups within the Canadian political system. If the downwardly mobile middle class sees more marginalized groups as the major threat to its economic security, the latter will inevitably lose in any struggle. Through its taxation policies and its presentation of the issues involved, the government is doing everything to encourage this response. In the end, this would constitute little more than a competition among victims, a struggle over a reduced number of seats in the lifeboat. If the struggle proceeds along such lines, Native people and other marginalized groups will be left to swim – or sink.

If, on the other hand, this segment of the middle class recognizes the nature of the process (and its own strategic position within it), the opportunity will exist for a different response. Because the middle class, too, is being squeezed in the same way, and if it realizes why it is being squeezed economically – to facilitate an increase in the concentration of wealth at the top – it may recognize how it, too, is being victimized by a long-term process destined to benefit others. In the process of recognizing this, the middle class might find new reasons for identifying with other victims of the same process: marginalized groups, including Native people. If it realizes how it is being manipulated politically, to provide the electoral support for a process to benefit the wealthy, it may become less willing to play the role assigned to it. A clearer recognition by the declining middle class of its position in the current political and economic conjuncture could provide the basis for a new degree of solidarity with Native people and other marginalized groups in Canada.

The Role of An Aboriginal Rights Coalition

If the current conditions provide an opportunity for greater solidarity between the middle class and marginalized groups, the question remains: What role could an inter-church coalition play in facilitating this potential solidarity?

The first and most obvious response would be to share the analysis. True solidarity arises out of situations where different groups discover their own reasons for wanting to achieve the same goals. The coming together of otherwise disparate groups on the basis of common interests provides the basis for true community. In the past, non-Natives were persuaded to become involved in Native issues largely on the basis of altruism. For whatever reason – conscience, guilt, Christian charity – they were willing to offer "support" to Native people when gross injustices appeared to be taking place. The underlying assumption still remained that Native problems were unrelated to their own, at least on a day-to-day basis. As long as this assumption held sway, the involvement of non-Natives remained limited to occasional offers of "support".

For solidarity to occur, it will be necessary for non-Native Canadians to discover their own reasons for reshaping Canadian society in ways that would also benefit Native people. Non-Natives have been encouraged to learn about the circumstances relating to Native people, but have seldom been encouraged to analyse their own. This can and must change if solidarity is to be developed, and if the government's long-term agenda is to be successfully challenged. No single group in society – the middle class, organized labour, Native people – can alter the Conservative/corporate agenda by acting on its own. Only by working with others toward a shared vision of an alterNative society can any single group hope to achieve its goals.

Fortunately, the conditions which could give rise to such critical reflection are increasingly apparent. The middle class – Project North's main constituency – is on the verge of being victimized by the same process threatening Native people, although in different ways. If the middle class can become aware of the factors contributing to its situation, and of the strategic role it can play in determining the outcome of the process affecting Native people and others, a new basis for solidarity could be developed.

The Aboriginal Rights Coalition (ARC), which replaced Project North in 1989, is in a unique position to facilitate this process of building solidarity. As an official church body, it has access to large church communities for educational work. Instead of merely trying to educate non-Natives about Native people and their concerns as in the past, ARC could use these opportunities to stimulate critical thinking in the middle class about its current circumstances, and the forces bearing down on it. This could be done through workshops at the local church or community level, with the backing of materials designed for "sharing the analysis". As it helps mainstream Canadians deal with their own circumstances, ARC could also identify the structural links between itself and Native people within the current conjuncture. In effect, ARC could help non-Native Canadians identify the basis for solidarity with aboriginal people.

At the same time as it works with non-Natives, ARC could also share its analysis with the many Native groups with which it has ties. Potentially, this could provide such groups with a basis for going beyond a mere defence of their own parochial concerns (a justifiable stance, given their history). If Native groups could be convinced that a number of other Canadians had reasons for wanting to significantly alter the status quo, they might be more inclined to enter into coalitions to develop a common vision and agenda. At a moment when the church, too, is suffering from a shrinking pot and is tempted to turn inwards and away from ecumenical social action projects such as ARC provide a solid basis which will address the church's own issues and those of the middle class as well.

ARC would also be in an excellent position to facilitate the process of coalition building. Communication links between Native and non-Native Canadians at the grassroots level are often poor, if they exist at all. The voices most often heard in the non-Native community are those in opposition to Native interests. By sharing its analysis with each sector, ARC could help establish the basis for a dialogue that would serve the interests of both sides. In cases of conflict between Natives and non-Natives over the use of resources, the conflict could be located within the broader trends in society, helping to overcome the "us versus them" mentality.

At the national level, ARC could play an instrumental role in the development of coalitions. The support of major church leaders for aboriginal issues has established a degree of credibility that would ensure easy access to national Native leaders. Beyond Native groups, ARC could also establish links with non-Native groups in the so-called "popular sector". A network of such groups has been building throughout the 1980s, and the analysis developed by ARC could augment their extensive efforts to develop a broad-based movement for social change in Canada.

ENDNOTES

1. Hon. John Munro, quoted in *Ottawa Citizen*, November 13, 1990.
2. *Indian and Native Programs, A Study Team Report to the Task Force on Program Review (The Nielsen Report)*. Minister of Supply and Services. (Ottawa: 1985).
3. John Calvert, *Government Limited*. (Ottawa: Canadian Centre for Policy AlterNatives), 1984, p. 105.
4. For an overview of this two-directional growth in government spending, see G. Bruce Doern et al., *Public Budgeting in Canada* (Ottawa: Carleton University Press, 1988), pp. 1-4. For a more detailed presentation of the State's evolving role in the post-WW II era, see David Wolfe, "The State and Economic Policy in Canada 1968-1975" in Leo Panitch, ed., *The Canadian State: Political Economy and Political Power* (Toronto: University of Toronto Press, 1977).
5. *Services and Subsidies to Business, A Study Team Report to the Task Force on Program Review*. Minister of Supply and Services. (Ottawa: 1985), p. 11. The list was broken down into two types of programs – those which provided subsidies and those which provided services to business. The breakdown was as follows: "The 57 subsidy programs cost a total of $4.5 billion in grants and contributions, and $7.7 billion in federal revenues, and directly involve 11,440 person-years. The 155 service programs cost $713 million in grants and contributions, $1,966 million in salaries, and $1,507 million in operations and maintenance costs; they directly involve 56,860 person- years of federal staff." (p.1)
6. Allan Moscovitch, "The Welfare State Since 1975." Occasional Papers Series, No. 3. (University of Regina: 1985), p. 2.
7. Cy Gonick, *The Great Economic Debate*. (Toronto: James Lorimer & Company, 1987), p. 299.
8. For a more detailed description of these trends in the post-war international economy and their impacts on Canada, see Wolfe, 1977 and Gonick, 1987.
9. For a detailed description of this new global economy, see Heather Menzies, *Fast Forward and Out of Control*. (Toronto: Macmillan of Canada, 1989), Chapter 2. This book should be on the "must read" list of every Canadian wishing to understand the critical forces shaping our society, especially the impact of technology.
10. For a succinct analysis of the historical stages of capitalism, see Joe Holland and Peter Henriot, *Social Analysis: Linking Faith and Justice*. (Maryknoll, N.Y.: Orbis Press, 1983), Chapter 4. This book should be of particular interest to Christians because it includes an analysis of how Roman Catholic church structures have evolved with stages of capitalism.
11. For a discussion of this "accommodation" between capital and labour, see Leo Panitch, "The Role and Nature of the Canadian State" in Panitch, 1977, especially pp. 20- 22.

78   AND THE LAST SHALL BE FIRST

12. The term "fiscal crisis" refers to a problem that is both economic and political in nature. On the economic level, it refers to the situation in which governments no longer have the revenue to match their expenses. On the political level, it describes the situation in which governments can no longer fulfil their political obligations: to the business sector on the one hand, and to the general public on the other.

For the seminal analysis of this phenomenon, see James O'Connor, *The Fiscal Crisis of the State*. (N.Y.: St. Martin's Press, 1973). O'Connor argues that all activities of advanced industrial states "must try to fulfil two basic and often mutually contradictory functions – accumulation and legitimation." (p. 6) In other words, they must maintain the conditions that will ensure the continued profitability of the private sector; at the same time, they must ensure the "loyalty and support" of the majority of citizens for social and economic arrangements that allow wealth to accumulate in private hands. Others (such as Panitch, 1977) have suggested a third function – coercion – which involves the use by the State "of its monopoly over the legitimate use of force to maintain or impose social order." (p. 8)

13. In his first budget as Finance Minister, John Turner reduced the top rate of corporate tax from 49 per cent to 40 per cent, effective Jan. 1, 1973. Wolfe, 1977, p. 271.

14. "Tax expenditures" refer to tax breaks or "loopholes" that allow an individual or corporation to pay less taxes than they would otherwise. In the government's words: "Such tax forgiveness . . . is equivalent to . . . first collecting the sums involved . . . and then making a direct expenditure or loan at an amount equal to the revenue foregone." Department of Finance, *Government of Canada Tax Expenditure Account*. (Ottawa: December, 1979), p. 1.

For an overview of trends relating to tax policy and tax expenditures, see Leon Muszynski, *Is It Fair?* (Ottawa: Canadian Centre for Policy Alternatives, 1988), Chapter 7; Calvert, 1984, Chapter 5; and especially Linda McQuaig, *Behind Closed Doors*. (Toronto: Penguin Books, 1987).

15. The loss of revenues through tax expenditures represents one of the major reasons for the rise in the deficit (the other being the rise in interest rates), yet there has been little public acknowledgement of it. The federal government has published a partial accounting of its tax expenditures on a few occasions (1979, 1980, and 1985) and each time, the cost of such expenditures was in the billions of dollars. In 1979, the Department of Finance reported that tax breaks for individuals alone had cost the federal treasury $13.8 billion in lost revenues – more than twice the amount of the deficit in that year. (Calvert, 1984), p. 97.

At least five OECD countries (Austria, France, Spain, the U.S., and West Germany) have laws which require that such accounts be published annually. (OECD is the Organisation for Economic Co-operation and Development.) In Canada, the Auditor General, the Standing Committee on Public Accounts, and the Senate Committee on Banking, Trade and Commerce have all called for the cost of tax expenditures to be publicly reported on a regular basis – to no avail.

16. The authors of the Nielsen Report on *Services and Subsidies to Business* were struck by the "different standards of accountability" associated with tax

breaks versus direct grants. They found that direct expenditure programs were controlled and monitored in accordance with strict "standards and cost-benefit methods developed by the Treasury Board." "Taxation," however, "is a different world." For one thing, "the quantum of money involved is often an order of magnitude greater." For another, "post hoc evaluation is as rare on tax measures as it is routine elsewhere." (p. 25).

There is much evidence to suggest that tax expenditures are ineffective at achieving their alleged goal – to stimulate investment and presumably create jobs. A study by one university economist indicated that "for every 21 cents of investment generated by tax breaks for manufacturers between 1972 and 1975, the Canadian treasury lost one dollar of tax revenue." *The Globe & Mail*, Feb. 6, 1984.

The government's own studies have confirmed that tax breaks are an ineffective tool for stimulating the economy. Comparing the impact of government initiatives on job creation, tax cuts were found to be the least effective. Arun S. Roy, "A Preliminary Report on Employment Impacts: Study of Employment Impacts of Alternative Government Initiatives and Related Criteria" done for the Labour Market Studies Division. *Employment & Immigration Canada*, 1984.

As new technologies take over increasing shares of the production process, it is clear that "job creation" can no longer be assumed to be the intended goal of tax incentives. As one economist put it: "Tax incentives which encourage companies to purchase new equipment can have the effect of replacing workers with machines." *The Globe & Mail*. (Feb. 6, 1984). On the relatively new phenomenon of "jobless economic growth," see Menzies, 1989, p. 29.

17. *The Globe & Mail*. (Nov. 7, 1984).

18. Moscovitch, 1985, p. 8. See also Moscovitch, "The Rise and Decline of the Canadian Welfare State" in *Perception*. (Nov.-Dec. 1982), pp. 26-28.

19. Department of Finance, Economic Review. (April 1985), p. 126.

20. *Ibid*. The proportion of the federal budget servicing the deficit rose from 12.2 per cent in 1970 to 16.2 per cent in 1980, and up to 19.3 per cent by 1982.

21. See McQuaig, 1987 for a detailed account of the notorious MacEachen budget of 1981. What made this budget so notorious was that it tried to rein in the billions of tax dollars lost each year through tax breaks – the benefits of which were enjoyed primarily by the wealthy.

According to McQuaig, the successful defeat of MacEachen's proposals was yet another demonstration of how the interests of a small but powerful segment of the population could take precedence over the majority of Canadians. In Chapter 5 of her book, she documents how an earlier attempt at progressive tax reform – the Carter Commission in the late 1960s – was also derailed by the political actions of the same elite group.

22. "The Prime Minister's Broadcasts to the Nation on the Economy." (Ottawa: Oct. 19-21, 1982).

23. Even as he was putting a cap on direct expenditures, the Minister of Finance, Marc Lalonde, admitted: "The increased federal deficit . . . was not due to runaway expenditure growth. It was due in large part to a succession of tax cuts introduced in response to weak activity." Department of Finance, *The Federal Deficit in Perspective*. (Ottawa: April 19, 1983), p. 8. In other words, the deficit

problem existed largely because the government had stopped collecting revenue to the extent it once had.

This analysis is borne out by statistics which show that while federal government expenditures remained steady at between 19 to 20 per cent of GNP throughout the last half of the 1970s, revenues during the same period declined from 20 per cent in 1974 to between 15 and 16 per cent of GNP by 1979. "The Federal Deficit and Universality of Social Programs" *Backgrounder* BP 202E, Library of Parliament (May 1989). The deficit was occurring not because the government was spending proportionately more than it had, but because it was collecting proportionately less in revenue.

The growth of tax expenditures during the 1970s largely accounted for this decline in revenue. The cost of borrowing money to make up the difference led to the rapid growth in government spending in the 1980s - a cost greatly exacerbated by the government's policy of high interest rates during the early part of the decade.

24. During its first term, the Mulroney government backed away from proposed changes to the unemployment insurance program, and from partially de-indexing old age pensions, but it did succeed in partially de-indexing family allowances and reducing its contributions to cost-shared programs with the provinces.

25. For an insider's account of the impact of this resistance on the Mulroney government, see Michel Gratton, *So What are the Boys Saying?* (Toronto: McGraw-Hill Ryerson, 1987), Chapter 12.

26. See Chapter 7, "Global Economics and the Decline of the Middle Class" in Menzies, 1989, pp. 198-228.

27. Department of Finance, *Economic Review*. (April, 1985), p. 124.

28. See McQuaig, 1987, Chapter 4, for a detailed account of the development of this "tax industry".

29. Department of Finance, *Budget Papers*. (February, 1986).

30. Muszynski, 1988, p. 41.

31. The principle of "targeting" public funds to "those most in need" is noticeably absent in discussions about tax breaks, even though such tax expenditures represent almost 40 per cent of government spending. There is much evidence to show that on the personal income tax level such tax breaks are highly regressive. According to figures released with MacEachen's 1981 budget, the average saving from all tax breaks for those with incomes between $10,000 - $15,000 was $771; for those with incomes above $100,000, the average saving was $46,000. (Cited in McQuaig, 1987, p. 222).

On the corporate side, as the authors of the *Nielsen Task Force Report* discovered (see note 15, above), there are almost no mechanisms to ensure that any benefits are derived from the billions of dollars of tax breaks handed out to businesses each year.

32. In 1982, the Liberals arbitrarily capped the increase in their contributions to cost-shared programs, under the "6 & 5" program. In 1985-86, the Conservatives announced plans to change the formula by which they shared the cost of health care and education in the provinces – changes that saved Ottawa more than $8 billion by 1992.

33. The signs of an organized backlash against the growing tax burden have been growing steadily throughout the 1980s. In April 1986, *The Toronto Sun* invited readers to write to the paper if they wanted "to protest the burden placed on middle income Canadians by the Government's recent budget." Forty thousand did so, and the results were delivered to the House of Commons. *Hansard* (April 16, 1988), p. 12307.

An organized attempt was made in Regina to elect a city council that would slash services to reduce the municipal tax burden. While this grassroots movement – spearheaded by the local business community – failed in its initial attempt, it could be repeated in other communities across Canada. The implementation of the GST could prove instrumental in further inciting this backlash.

34. As another example of how regressive tax expenditures can be, the National Council of Welfare noted that taxpayers with incomes above $250,000 enjoyed 25 per cent of the benefits from the capital gains tax exemption, although they represented only one per cent of people who filed taxes. Their average benefit from this one tax break was $20,628, while those with incomes between $20,000 and $30,000 gained an average of only $147. "Testing Tax Reform," A Brief to the Standing Committee on Finance and Economic Affairs, *National Council of Welfare*. (Ottawa: September, 1987).

35. Figures taken from "Social Security and Social Welfare Legislation in Canada," Library of Parliament *Backgrounder*. (April, 1989). The threshold level for the Sales Tax Credit was raised to $16,000 in 1988.

36. E. Richard Shillington, "Inflation Taxes" in *The Ottawa Citizen*. (March 7, 1990), p. A9.

37. According to the *National Council of Welfare* (1987), tax deductions for RRSP contributions "reward those who least need a government subsidy at an annual cost of over $2 billion." (p. 5). Since coming to power, the Conservatives have steadily increased the amount that can be contributed each year to an RRSP.

38. *Pro-Canada Dossier* #23. (Jan. 1, 1990).

39. See *Pro-Canada Dossier* #18 (Dec. 16, 1989) for a detailed analysis of the voting patterns which contributed to the Conservatives' re-election, although a majority of Canadians opposed the Free Trade Agreement (FTA). No consideration of the election is complete without reference to the strategic role played by the business community in the final days of the campaign.

40. *The Globe & Mail*. (March 30, 1989). According to the analysis of an Environics poll, the Conservatives "continued to do well" among this sector, which "propelled them to electoral victory."

41. Statement of the Government of Canada on Indian Policy (1969).

42. Since coming to power in 1984, the Conservative government has transferred responsibility for forestry management, mine safety, health services, and energy utilities to the N.W.T. and Yukon. See "Notes for Remarks by the Hon. Bill McKnight, Minister of DIAND, to the 11th National Northern Development Conference." (Edmonton: Oct. 26, 1988).

43. *Indian and Native Programs*. (Nielsen Report, 1985), pp. 10-12.

44. Memorandum to Cabinet, *Report of the Ministerial Task Force on Native Programs*. (April 12, 1985).

45. *Ibid.*, p. 1.
46. *Ibid.*, p. 7.
47. *Nielsen Report*, p. 21.
48. *Ibid.*, p. 22.
49. *Memorandum to Cabinet*, 1985, p. 15.
50. *Ibid.*, p. 16.
51. *Ibid.*, p. 14.
52. *Ibid.*, p. 31.
53. *House of Commons, Standing Committee on Aboriginal Affairs and Northern Development.* (June 23, 1988).
54. *Ibid.*
55. Letter from Chartered Accountant Norman Hawkins to the office of Keith Penner M.P. (May 18, 1988).
56. House of Commons *Hansard*. (March 17, 1988), pp. 13859-60.
57. For a detailed and eloquent portrayal of these struggles, see Boyce Richardson, ed., *Drum Beat: Anger and Renewal in Indian Country*. (Toronto: Summerhill Press, 1989).
58. *Regina Leader-Post*. (Nov. 8, 1989).
59. *Ottawa Citizen*. (July 8, 1987), p. 4.
60. The duplicity exhibited by Canada's First Ministers deserves to be highlighted. The negotiations leading to the Meech Lake Accord were going on at the same time as the preparations for the First Ministers' Conference on Aboriginal Rights. The premiers who were arguing on principle against any open-ended recognition of the right to self-government were at the same time engaged in the negotiations which led to the recognition of Quebec as a "distinct society."
61. "Native Law in a Nutshell," a presentation by David Knoll, Federation of Saskatchewan Indian Nations, to a Native Law Conference in Saskatoon. (March 7, 1987), p. 17.
62. Statement of the Government of Canada on Indian Policy (1969), cited in Brad Morse, ed., *Aboriginal Peoples and the Law*. (Ottawa: Carleton University Press, 1985), p. 618. While the intent of the White Paper was to "free" Native people from the constraints associated with their separate legal status, the policy proposals would have had the effect of "freeing" the federal government from innumerable responsibilities: legal, constitutional, economic and political.
63. The government did appoint an Indian Claims Commissioner, Dr. Lloyd Barber, in December 1969, but according to Knoll, 1987, his Commission was "discredited as a creature of the White Paper" (p. 7). Barber's initial mandate was only to "receive and study the grievances" Indians might still have against the government, and to "recommend measures" to the Government of Canada on how those claims could be discharged. (Cited in Morse, 1985, p. 627). In 1971, his mandate was expanded to allow him to examine claims based on unextinguished aboriginal title. With little power of its own, the Commission was not in a position to resolve any of the problems it identified. The Land Claims Commission was quietly dissolved in 1977.

64. *Ibid.*, pp. 620-621.

65. For an in-depth account of the process which led up to the 1969 White Paper, see Sally Weaver, *Making Canadian Indian Policy.* (Toronto: University of Toronto Press, 1981). For a more general presentation of this period, see James S. Frideres, *Native Peoples in Canada: Contemporary Conflicts*, 3rd ed. (Scarborough: Prentice-Hall Canada Inc., 1988), pp. 124- 127.

66. The most far-reaching court ruling was the 1973 Supreme Court of Canada decision on *Calder v. Attorney General of British Columbia* which affirmed for the first time the possibility that Natives who had never signed treaties could still be in possession of their full aboriginal rights – the exact meaning of which had yet to be determined. Other significant, short-lived, legal victories obtained by Natives in the early 1970s included the successful application in 1972 by the Dene to file a caveat (a declaration of legal interest) on unpatented Crown lands in the N.W.T., and the injunction obtained by the James Bay Cree to stop, at least temporarily, the proposed flooding of their lands. For a more detailed overview of these rulings, see Morse, 1985.

67. "Statement on Claims of Indian and Inuit People," Department of Indian Affairs and Northern Development Press Release. (Aug. 8, 1973).

68. The official name of this department has evolved over the years. For the sake of consistency, DIAND is used throughout.

69. State of the Government of Canada on Indian Policy (1969). Cited in Morse, 1985, p. 618.

70. Frideres, 1988, p. 99.

71. *Ibid.*, p. 99.

72. "Specific Claims Policy and Process," a submission to the Liberal Party of Canada Policy Forum on Aboriginal and First Nations Issues by the Treaty & Aboriginal Rights Research Centre of Manitoba. (April, 1986), p. 2.

73. Cited in Morse, 1985, p. 634.

74. Knoll, 1985, p. 16.

75. In a landmark ruling, the Supreme Court of Canada declared in *Guerin v. The Queen* (1984) that the Crown's trust responsibility toward Indians and their lands was legally enforceable, meaning the government could be sued for damages if it failed to act in the best interests of the Indians. Prior to this decision, the government had always insisted that its trust responsibilities toward Indians were political only, and therefore not enforceable in the courts.

76. To illustrate this point, the Treaty and Aboriginal Rights Research Centre of Manitoba has cited the case of two bands in Manitoba that received separate and different opinions from the Department of Justice about when their reserves came into existence – a crucial point in determining the validity of subsequent surrenders of reserve lands. One band was told its reserve did not legally exist until an order-in-council was passed. The other was told by a different Justice lawyer that this was not a necessary precondition for its reserve to be created. For more details, see "Specific Claims Policy and Processes", a discussion paper produced by the T.A.R.R. Centre of Manitoba. (April, 1986).

77. Indian and Northern Affairs Canada *Annual Report.* (1985 - 86), p. 15.

84 AND THE LAST SHALL BE FIRST

78. Stony Rapids in 1981, and Fond Du Lac in 1986.

79. *"Living Treaties: Lasting Agreements"*, Report of the Task Force to Review Comprehensive Land Claims Policy. (Ottawa: 1985).

80. Cited in *Regina Leader-Post*. (Nov. 7, 1989), p. A5.

81. *The Globe & Mail*. (March 25, 1989), p. B10.

82. Andrew Nikiforuk and Ed Struzik, "The Great Forest Sell-Off" in *Report on Business Magazine, The Globe & Mail*. (Nov. 1989), p. 59.

83. *Ottawa Citizen*. (March 3, 1990).

84. *Ibid.*

85. Nikiforuk and Struzik, 1989, p. 61.

86. Boyce Richardson, "Wrestling With the Canadian System: A Decade of Lubicon Frustration", in *Drumbeat*, pp. 229-264.

87. *Ibid.*, p. 254.

88. Daniel Ashini, "David Confronts Goliath: The Innu of Ungava versus the NATO Alliance", in *Drumbeat*, p. 60.

89. *Ibid.*, p. 64.

90. Fr. Alexis Jouveneau, speaking to the Federal Environmental Assessment Review Panel, cited in *Drumbeat*, p. 63.

91. Jim Fulton M.P., *Skeena Report*. (Summer, 1989), p. 11.

92. CBC Mackenzie Regional News. (Oct. 4, 1989).

93. *The Vancouver Sun*. (Oct. 14, 1989).

94. *Canadian Lawyer*. (October, 1989), pp. 14-15. The article noted: "Native land claims pushed fallout from bank failures, urea formaldehyde lawsuits, and even free trade out of the spending spotlight for outside legal services during Ottawa's most recent fiscal period (April 1, 1988 - March 31, 1989)."

95. "Letter to the People of Canada" from Don Ryan, President of the Gitksan-Wet'suwet'en Tribal Council (May 25, 1988).

96. Prime Minister Pierre Trudeau: Remarks on Aboriginal and Treaty Rights. Excerpts from a speech given Aug. 8, 1969, in Vancouver. Trudeau stated: "But aboriginal rights, this really means saying, 'We were here before you. You came and you took the land from us and perhaps you cheated us by giving us some worthless things in return for vast expanses of land and we want to re-open this question. We want to preserve our aboriginal rights and to restore them to us.' And our answer is . . .'no.'"

97. Canadian Press, March 27, 1990.

98. Assembly of First Nations *Bulletin*. (June 1988), p. 1.

INDEX

aboriginal rights 24, 35-37, 46, 48, 51, 59, 60, 63, 65, 66, 72, 74, 75
Aboriginal Rights Coalition 74, 75
Algonquin 33
Alternative Funding Arrangements 33
Amazon 51-53
Assembly of First Nations (AFN) 30, 31, 64
Bear Island 33, 58
Calder 45, 59
capital 8, 9, 11, 13, 14, 28-30
capitalism 8
child tax credit 15
"clawback" 18
comprehensive claims 29, 38, 39, 41, 44, 48-50, 61
Conservatives 2, 3, 11-18, 24, 28-30, 38, 41-44, 48-51, 63
constitution 2, 35, 36, 60, 63, 65, 72
Coolican Report 44, 49, 50
COPE 11, 34, 47
corporate agenda 16-18, 31, 73, 75
corporate taxes 10, 13, 14
deficit 11, 12, 15-18, 31
Dene 32, 44-47
Dene Declaration 46
Department of Justice 29, 39-41, 57, 61
DIAND 27-29, 39, 40, 48
"downloading" 14
First Ministers' Conference 66
fiscal crisis 7, 9, 11, 13-15, 24, 32, 34, 36
fiscal restraint 3, 24, 30
forestry 52, 53
Forget Commission 12
Free Trade Agreement 16, 18, 73
G.N.W.T. 47
Georges Erasmus 30, 31, 64
Gitksan-Wet'suwet'en 58, 60
Goods and Services Tax 18

government spending 7, 8, 14, 23, 25
Haida 33
hydro-electric development 53
ideology of restraint 10
In All Fairness 41
incentives 9, 10
Innu 55, 56
international division of labour 8
Inuit 1, 26, 27, 30, 35, 44-47, 51, 56
Inuit Tapirisat of Canada 30
investment capital 9
James Bay Cree 31
Keynes 7
labour 8, 9, 13, 31, 75
land entitlement claims 43
lawful obligation 39-41
Lubicon 33, 34, 54, 55, 57
Mackenzie Valley 47, 56, 72
McKnight, Bill 29, 49
Meech Lake Accord 37, 65
Métis 1, 32, 35, 44, 68
Micmacs 33, 61, 62
middle class 1, 3, 13-16, 18, 71-76
militarization 55
Mulroney, Brian 11, 29, 65
Nielsen Report on Indians and Natives 2
Nielsen Report on Services and Subsidies to Business 7
Nisga'a 31, 59, 60
Nunavut 46, 47
Office of Native Claims 39, 41, 42
oil and gas development 54
Outstanding Business 41
Pro-Canada Network 31
Project North 71-73, 75
Royal Proclamation 59, 67, 68
Saskatchewan Formula 42, 44
self-government 2, 24, 29-34, 37, 42, 63, 66
social programs 7, 9-16, 18, 73
South Moresby 34
specific claims 38, 39, 41, 42, 44, 63

subsidies 7, 10, 17, 47
Supreme Court of Canada 45, 58, 59, 61, 62, 67
tax expenditures 10, 15
tax revenues 8
Third World 8, 55
Trudeau, Pierre 36, 67
Unemployment Insurance 7, 8, 11, 12, 18
universality 11, 15, 18, 19
White Paper 23, 38, 39, 63, 64
Wilson, Michael 14, 30
Yukon 24, 32, 44, 45, 59, 67
Yukon Indians 44, 45